SMALL and MIGHTY

Conversations about small schools

Aimée Tinkler
With a foreword by Mary Myatt

Together we unlock every learner's unique potential

At Hachette Learning (formerly Hodder Education), there's one thing we're certain about. No two students learn the same way. That's why our approach to teaching begins by recognising the needs of individuals first.

Our mission is to allow every learner to fulfil their unique potential by empowering those who teach them. From our expert teaching and learning resources to our digital educational tools that make learning easier and more accessible for all, we provide solutions designed to maximise the impact of learning for every teacher, parent and student.

Aligned to our parent company, Hachette Livre, founded in 1826, we pride ourselves on being a learning solutions provider with a global footprint.

www.hachettelearning.com

Although every effort has been made to ensure that website addresses are correct at time of going to press, Hachette Learning cannot be held responsible for the content of any website mentioned in this book. It is sometimes possible to find a relocated web page by typing in the address of the home page for a website in the URL window of your browser.

Hachette UK's policy is to use papers that are natural, renewable and recyclable products and made from wood grown in well-managed forests and other controlled sources. The logging and manufacturing processes are expected to conform to the environmental regulations of the country of origin.

To order, please visit www.HachetteLearning.com or contact Customer Service at education@hachette.co.uk / +44 (0)1235 827827.

ISBN: 978 1 0360 0269 5

© Aimée Tinkler, 2025

First published in 2025 by
Hachette Learning, (a trading division of Hodder & Stoughton Limited),
An Hachette UK Company
Carmelite House
50 Victoria Embankment
London EC4Y 0DZ
www.HachetteLearning.com

The authorised representative in the EEA is Hachette Ireland, 8 Castlecourt Centre, Dublin 15, D15 XTP3, Ireland (email: info@hbgi.ie)

Impression number   10 9 8 7 6 5 4 3 2 1
Year   2029 2028 2027 2026 2025

All rights reserved. Apart from any use permitted under UK copyright law, no part of this publication may be reproduced or transmitted in any form or by any means, electronic or mechanical, including photocopying and recording, or held within any information storage and retrieval system, without permission in writing from the publisher or under licence from the Copyright Licensing Agency Limited. Further details of such licences (for reprographic reproduction) may be obtained from the Copyright Licensing Agency Limited, www.cla.co.uk

Cover photo: Shutterstock
Typeset in the UK.
Printed in the UK.

A catalogue record for this title is available from the British Library.

For my Dad, whose quiet encouragement and faith in my ideas make every project feel possible.

Aimée Tinkler has been a teacher for 25 years during which time she has taught and led in schools in a variety of circumstances and contexts. Aimée has become an advocate for small and rural schools after spending 10 years teaching and leading in very small schools in rural Derbyshire. Aimée has worked with many organisations across the wider sector in an advisory capacity and is closely involved with the work of the Chartered College of Teaching where she is president and a founding fellow. Aimée is engaged in doctoral research at UCL Institute of Education and has published research with several organisations across the sector.

ACKNOWLEDGEMENTS

This book would not have been possible without the generosity and insight of so many people who contributed along the way. My thanks go to everyone who shared their expertise, experiences, and time so willingly.

To colleagues working in small schools across the country, thank you for everything you do. The work you carry out every day is an inspiration, and this book is a testament to your commitment.

To my family, thank you for your patience and support. It's fitting that my children are themselves the product of small schools – a living reminder of the impact that close-knit communities can have on shaping confident, capable, and kind individuals. You've been my biggest cheerleaders, tea-makers, and occasional editors, and I wouldn't have managed this without you.

Thank you to my great friend Jackie, who is the ultimate finisher – proofreading and spellchecking every word with care. Your attention to detail and support have been invaluable.

Finally, I want to thank Mary Myatt for her encouragement and inspiration. Your belief that our schools are indeed small and mighty has shone a light on their brilliance and uniqueness. Your insight has been a driving force behind this project, and your support has helped to highlight everything that makes small schools so remarkable.

This is a collective effort, and I'm grateful to all of you for being part of it.

CONTENTS

Foreword by Mary Myatt ix

Introduction xi

1 Jo Luxford - Leading Across Schools: Managing Teams and Transforming Small Communities 1

2 Claire Bills - Lessons in Leadership: Growing Through the Opportunities of Small School Headship 7

3 Dave Ellison-Lee - Empowering Small Schools: Trust-wide Support and Collaboration 13

4 Alex Pethick – Aspiring for Excellence: Designing Ambitious Curricula in Small Schools 21

5 Katie Fitzsimmons - Small Schools Through a Diocesan Lens: Support, Challenges, and Opportunities 29

6 Kirsty Cooper - Belonging and Justice: Creating a Vision for Small Schools 37

7 Neil Dixon – Supporting Small Schools: A Trust's Role in Sustaining Community and Excellence 45

8 Cassie Young – Inclusive by Design: Building SEND Excellence in Small Schools 51

9 Mary Carey – Islands of Learning: Teaching Remote School Communities 59

10 Phil Banks - Small Schools: A Hub of Connection, Belonging, and Community 69

11 Katy Chedzey – Shaping Practice – Engaging with Research in Small School Settings 79

12 Victoria Gascoyne-Cecil – Thriving Together: Supporting SEND Learners in Small Schools.. 87

13 Ed Finch - From Moorland Challenges to Community Connections: Leading a Rural Small School...95

14 Jacqueline Bone - Teaching in Mixed-Age Infant Classes: Challenges, Strategies, and Rewards... 103

15 Jennie Gill – Learning Across Ages: Maximising Opportunities in Mixed-age Classrooms...109

16 Neil Short - Advocating for Small Schools: The Role and Impact of the National Association of Small Schools 119

17 Michael Allen - Stepping Into Leadership: Experiences and Insights From a New Leader in a Small School...127

Glossary of Acronyms and Abbreviations...131

FOREWORD

What struck me most about this wonderful book is that while there are innumerable challenges running, working and supporting small schools, there's also a vibrancy and energy from so many colleagues working in this part of the sector. This isn't to be Pollyanna-ish or sentimental; rather, it's a hard-nosed observation that colleagues working in and supporting small schools have both much to celebrate and plenty for other parts of the sector to learn from. I truly believe there are insights here that we can all reflect on.

There are two aspects to *Small and Mighty*: the first is to celebrate schools' unique characteristics and the fizz they bring to children and their communities. The second is that everyone, wherever they work in the sector, can take something from this collection of conversations, reflect on it and possibly apply it to their own practice.

I found the same in the conversations I had for *SEND Huh*. For instance, Gary Aubin's terrific metaphor that we might consider an inclusive curriculum through the metaphor of a set of automatic doors: useful for all and essential for some. While this was a conversation related to Gary's work in SEND, I make the case that this insight is something we can all reflect on. Each chapter in *Small and Mighty* offers a glimpse into the extraordinary efforts dedicated to providing a rich curriculum, and to teaching children, a testament to the deep-seated role that small schools play in their communities.

By way of example, everyone would gain something from Jo Luxford's observation: 'We all know that school can be much more than the place our children spend their time, or where they learn to read and write. Working in a tiny school brings that into focus in a way that I'd not experienced before.' And we might all reflect on this, from Jennie Gill: 'I have known three of my predecessors in my classroom and between us we span most of the last 60 years. They have passed on to me a legacy of respect and goodwill for the role that they worked hard to achieve. This level of 'knowing' and 'being known' in a community brings both great privilege and great responsibility. There are also fascinating accounts of how to make small schools work at scale – for example, Dave Ellison-Lee's account of how his trust supports curriculum development, professional learning and sense of community across 26 schools, 13 of which are below one form entry. Again, we might all reflect on how some of these ways of working might influence our practice, even though we are in a different part of the sector.

There are terrific examples of how to plan and teach the curriculum in mixed-age classes. For example, Alex Pethick's account of how she supports schools to sequence what children need to learn, over more than one year, is immensely helpful for anyone planning a curriculum. In a small school, every child is more than a name on a register, they are individuals known by their teachers, peers, and families. What we glean from the interviews is that the educators and leaders within these schools are not just teachers—they are mentors, advocates, and often lifelines for families.

However, the challenges faced by small schools cannot be understated. Limited resources, the need for multifaceted roles and the pressure of meeting diverse educational needs can be overwhelming.

Yet, even with these constraints there's tremendous ingenuity and determination: their voices in these chapters show how collaboration and creativity can transform obstacles into opportunities.

Anyone reading this will find invaluable insights into innovative practices, the importance of fostering a culture of belonging, and the significance of community engagement. The stories not only celebrate the victories of small schools but also challenge us to recognise the value they hold within the broader educational landscape.

Mary Myatt

INTRODUCTION

Anyone who has taught or led in a small primary school knows that while they exist, like all schools, to educate children and serve their communities, life in small schools is different. For almost half of my teaching career so far, I have had the privilege of teaching and serving as a school leader in small schools, and those years, while immensely rewarding, have demonstrated just how challenging this endeavour can be.

Small schools are often the beating heart of their communities, places where every child is known by name, every family feels personally connected and every staff member plays a vital, multifaceted role. However, behind the warmth of these close-knit environments lies the reality of limited resources, tight budgets, and the constant need to adapt to ever-changing demands. Working in a small school requires a unique combination of flexibility, innovation, and resilience—qualities that small school practitioners demonstrate on a daily basis.

This book brings together the voices of those who understand these joys and challenges best: the teachers, leaders, and staff who work in small schools. Through a series of interviews, these practitioners share their firsthand experiences—the triumphs, the struggles, and the creative solutions they've found to ensure their schools continue to thrive. Their stories offer a window into the complexities of leading and teaching in small schools, where the constraints of size often give rise to remarkable ingenuity and community spirit.

The interviews presented here are more than just reflections on the challenges small schools face; they are a celebration of the unique strengths of these environments. From fostering deep relationships with students and families to finding ways to deliver a broad curriculum with fewer resources, these practitioners reveal the heart and soul of small school life. Their insights show how, even in the face of adversity, small schools can achieve extraordinary things through collaboration, dedication, and a shared commitment to their children.

It has been a privilege to speak to colleagues across the country and I hope the stories in this book inspire other to appreciate the incredible work being done in these vibrant, resilient communities.

LEADING ACROSS SCHOOLS: MANAGING TEAMS AND TRANSFORMING SMALL COMMUNITIES

A conversation with Jo Luxford

Jo Luxford is hub principal of four tiny schools in rural North Devon: Bridgerule C of E Primary School, Bradford Primary School and Nursery, Black Torrington C of E Primary School and Highampton Primary School. Jo also leads on the Early Years Foundation Stage across the 14 primary schools in her trust and is chair of governors for a cluster of three small schools in another local trust. Jo has taught in schools of all sizes but has developed a real passion for championing the relevance of small schools both in terms of their roles in village and rural communities and of their place in the educational landscape of the UK.

Twitter/X @joannapple

> *Small schools are ideal places for research, innovation and development; in teaching and learning, curriculum development, leadership and for developing quality practice in education through collaboration and partnership. Small schools are connected with, central to and assets for communities through their influential relationships with pupils, parents and extended families and as such provide opportunities for adult learning, developments in technology and sustainability.*
>
> **Dr Cath Gristy and Neil Short, *Small Schools Manifesto* (2022)***

---

* Can be found at https://smallschools.org.uk/small-schools-manifesto

Please can you tell us about your current role and your experience working with small schools?

My own teaching experience from 2001 to 2017 was predominantly in fairly standard, two- or three-form entry, first and primary schools where I taught in Reception, Year 1 and Year 2 over the years, including 10 years part time while I raised my three children. I became fascinated by tiny schools when we moved to Devon and my children attended our two-class local village school of around 30 pupils. The village school community was a lifeline for me as a young mum of three in a relatively isolated area and I threw myself into school and village life. When the opportunity came up to interview for the job of Reception/Year 1/Year 2 class teacher at the same school I took it. I had to do some soul searching as my youngest son was just entering Year 2 so I would be teaching him, but I went for it and have not looked back. Over the next couple of years, the school went through some changes, with both the head of school and the administrator off work for long periods. This was a bit of a 'boot camp' for me. I learned ropes I hadn't previously even known existed! The job was exhilarating, gruelling and bonkers but I found it more rewarding than any job I'd held before. There was something about the privilege of building relationships with a close-knit community of families, and of being hands-on with both EYFS induction and Year 6 leavers that made the whole primary journey make sense in a way it hadn't previously. We all know that school can be much more than the place our children spend their time, or where they learn to read and write. Working in a tiny school brings that into focus in a way that I'd not experienced before.

Following this experience, at the start of 2022 I was asked by my trust lead to take on an associate principal role at two tiny schools. Two schools became three at the start of 2023 and from September 2023, when we moved to a hub model as a trust, a fourth school was added to my hub. The Dartmoor area has a lot of tiny village schools. My trust has three small school hubs encompassing 12 schools, so I work alongside the other hub principals closely.

Can you tell us more about each of your schools and how they are structured?

The largest of my schools has around 80 pupils in three classes plus a popular nursery. The classes are currently Reception and Years 1/2, 3/4 and 5/6. I have an associate principal based there, who has an 0.5 teaching load and works as maths lead across the hub.

The next largest has 30 pupils in two classes, Reception and Years 1/2 and Years 3/4/5/6. My lead teacher is based there, he has an 0.6 class responsibility and works across the hub including as reading lead over the three smaller schools.

The next smallest has a role of only 23, but the nursery that we started only last year is already popular and growing. We currently take children from two years old but plan to take children from nine months in the very near future. Growing this provision is one of the projects I am most excited about at the moment.

Finally, my smallest school that draws the most shocked intakes of breath – it currently has eight children on role! As an historically very small, village church school, we are completely committed to keeping it open for business so we are exploring innovative ways to do this in a way that is educationally and socially viable. Currently, the children are taught in one class by an amazing teacher job-share and an equally amazing HLTA. They travel frequently to Bradford in the afternoons for shared lessons and social time.

What are the benefits of having an executive principal across four schools?

I think on paper the greatest benefit for the school is obviously around saving money. The cost of employing me is spread over the four schools which makes it affordable in a way it definitely wouldn't be otherwise. If we are to keep our smallest schools open and thriving, then we have to make every penny of precious tax-payers money work as hard as it can. Combining multiple, very small, schools to create the equivalent of a smallish single school is a solution that can work. We also share an administrator over the four schools, and lots of the other operational aspects of school life are centralised in our trust. We have worked hard to make these aspects of school life work for us. I love a system, so we rely a lot on those.

Secondly, I think an executive headteacher post can have a manageable, if complex, leadership-focussed work pattern. Traditionally, small school heads have part-time class teaching responsibilities, which I feel brings a range of problems, even if you can recruit to the role! I have been a class teacher recently enough to know that the job is all-consuming, and it doesn't really leave time or headspace for the work of leading and running a school. It is also the case that although it is completely possible to schedule the strategic aspects of leadership into a two-day release arrangement, often, unfortunately, safeguarding issues, operational issues and general day-to-day dramas don't behave themselves and occur on your non-teaching days! By being non-class based, I am flexible enough to be able to deal with the inevitable as well as being able to maintain focus on the strategic work. I teach some PPA cover sessions which means I keep my hand in, but these are flexible enough to fit into my week. Typically, I spend the equivalent of a day a week in each school, plus a day for trust level EYFS work. In practice this looks like two-half days in each school, with lots of popping in and out *en route*, and the EYFS work fits in around things. My schools are within a 20-minute drive of one another, with the three smaller schools being within 10 minutes. I travel a lot, but I feel it is important to be present and visible and I make calls and voice notes a lot while I drive, so it isn't wasted time.

Easily the biggest benefit of the executive leadership model for me is around having a diverse and broad team of people working across the schools. Small school headship can be a lonely and overwhelming job but as an executive head I have an actual senior leadership team! Over the four schools I have an associate principal, a lead teacher and an assistant SENCO, all of whom teach part time. We share a SENCO with another hub. This group of incredible people share both the day-to-day responsibilities for running the schools and the strategic school improvement work with me. I believe that if tiny schools are to be sustainable in the long run, we need to find creative ways to create teams of talented, skilled and dedicated people and not rely on one individual to shoulder everything alone.

Finally, I think the schools can benefit in the same way, from working as part of a bigger team across more than one site. There is more support, a wider range of expertise and opportunities for collaboration and sharing – something that teachers are so good at but that can be tricky in small schools.

Does working as a group of schools have benefits for the teachers in terms of professional development?

I believe that teachers are naturally curious, hungry to learn and develop and absolute experts in creative problem solving. Teachers benefit from all kinds of opportunities to collaborate and share, and one of the joys of my current role has been really working to develop robust systems and processes around team-working over multiple sites. For example, we have reduced the number of staff meetings and made the remaining ones a bit longer, plus allowed travel time, so we can meet in person as a whole team at one of the schools regularly. The power in collaborative planning and moderation is so worth it. I love it in a staff meeting when I can see teachers from across the schools challenging, supporting and inspiring one another. We have also created a shared digital space, where everyone can see and collaborate on almost all of the documents we use, from planning to resources to risk assessments.

The hub model we use also shares subject leadership responsibilities over the four sites, so a subject lead benefits from a bit more to get their teeth into, the chance to work with a wider group of peers and the space to focus on one subject rather than multiple subject lead roles (up to six, sometimes), which is what subject leadership looked like in stand-alone small schools when I started out. I think this is brilliant for career progression and building confidence as well as expertise.

I hold to the idea that teaching in a small school is basically leadership bootcamp and actively encourage my teams to attribute value to the things they think nothing of doing on a daily basis. They are all skilled at dealing with parents, safeguarding issues, behaviour; you name it, they do it. There needs to be a shift in how teachers see themselves from 'I just work in a village school' to 'I basically run a school'. The job has built in professional development, we just need our teachers to recognise it.

We know that small-school teachers have complex roles demanding a lot of time, how do you ensure teachers are able to stay up to date with the latest research around pedagogy and practice?

I don't think I have found the solution to this, but I do have a few strategies that can at least help. I think it is all about attempting to create a culture where keeping up with research is what you just do. So, firstly I try to always reference research – the EEF (Educational Endowment Foundation) is great for bitesize stuff – in every staff meeting, in pupil progress meetings, in my weekly team newsletters and just in conversations. I also try to give pre-reading for staff meetings or, if possible, pre-listening of a relevant podcast. Secondly, I have spent a little bit of precious budget on a small CPD library which I rotate around the schools, and I always take in my copies of *Impact* and leave them around! I love the bit in the *Small Schools Manifesto*, above, which talks about how small schools are ideal places for research and innovation. Finally, I think there is work to be done in changing the narrative around small schools, not just in the way others see us, but in the way we see ourselves. Yes, we wear a lot of hats, but there are aspects of small school life that are easier than those of our colleagues in big, city schools so we can't let ourselves off the hook too readily. We need to stop seeing ourselves as behind the times and lean into the idea that we can actually be ahead of the curve! We can be so agile; we can explore and implement new ideas quickly, can measure their impact easily and can try things a bigger school would struggle with, without making huge waves.

Do you have any advice for leaders in small schools who are aware of the evidence base around what makes great teaching but also face the challenges and complexities of very busy small school life?

I really don't think there is any such place as a school that isn't challenging and complex, no matter the size. There are aspects of 'great teaching' that are clearly universal, and we need to make sure we are focussed on getting these down in our small schools as in the bigger ones. No-one could argue that the knottier aspects – very mixed-age classrooms, tiny cohorts, larger representation of children with SEND – are not a challenge in tiny schools but if we remember that we're all on a journey, and make a conscious effort to travel with an attitude of hope, curiosity and humility, then we have a good chance of getting to where we need to go. My only advice would be to network. Don't accept isolation, push yourself to raise your eyes from the day-to-day. Reach out and surround yourself with other leaders in a similar position. There are amazing groups on X, WhatsApp; the NASS (National Association of Special Schools) is excellent; there are small-school-specific training opportunities, particularly through the Church of England but also elsewhere; your work has made sure that the small schools agenda is heard in the Chartered College. You might not agree with everyone, you might not be in the exact same situation, but if we want to give children from our rural and coastal communities access to the very best, evidence-based teaching then we have a much better chance of getting it right if we collaborate.

LESSONS IN LEADERSHIP: GROWING THROUGH THE OPPORTUNITIES OF SMALL SCHOOL HEADSHIP

A conversation with Claire Bills

> Claire Bills is an experienced educator with 16 years in the field, currently in her seventh year as a head teacher. Her diverse background spans from large three-form entry schools in Nottingham City to smaller, four-class rural schools in Nottinghamshire. Claire has worked in various educational settings, including community and church schools, where her faith has significantly shaped her leadership approach. Now in her second year as head teacher at a 1.5-form entry primary school in Nottinghamshire, Claire is committed to integrating the close-knit, personal touch of smaller schools into her new, larger setting.

Please could you tell us a bit more about your journey from being a head teacher in a small school to a head teacher in a bigger school?

I moved to be head of a small primary school six years ago. Our school was a trust school in a rural Nottinghamshire village with 115 children on roll with four mixed-age classes. Prior to taking up the post, I had got to a point in my career where I was quite frustrated by the leadership of the school I worked in and I decided that the way to change a culture is to be the one that sets it. I decided to take on a headship. I absolutely loved it. I loved everything about being in a small school, I felt like I was part of a community very quickly. I had an amazing deputy head teacher, and we co-lead the school together. It was just such a joyful and encouraging role to come alongside someone who had so much potential and so much skill. She took the headship when I left, and I couldn't be more delighted. My current school is much bigger. We are a one-and-a-half form entry, there are many more staff and I now have a full senior leadership team.

It's clear that you enjoyed your role as head of a small school. Why did you decide to look for a headship in a bigger school?

I loved being head of that school. I loved every single child, and I knew the families really well. My biggest issue was that over time, I just found the financial model more and more difficult to work within. The way that we were supporting the children with the resources we had just wasn't sustainable. That really upset me quite deeply, I felt that we were less and less able to meet the increasing needs of the children because we were so limited by so many things. A personal driver for me is that I have always needed to work in a school where I know we are offering children the absolute best. At the start of my headship, I was really confident that every child was getting as good, if not a better, quality of education than a child in any of the larger schools nearby. That mattered. When I showed a prospective parent around I could say with absolute integrity, 'If you choose us, I can promise you we will be able to offer your child an outstanding quality of education'. Over time I became less certain that I could offer that guarantee under the restrictions we faced.

A number of families chose our school because of our small size. Often this was because their children had additional needs, but sometimes just because they thought they would be better suited to a smaller school environment. There were two bigger schools on either side of us graded by Ofsted as outstanding, but for some families, we really were best placed to meet their children's needs. We developed a reputation where parents felt confident that their child was going to be known, loved and valued exactly as they were. As a new pupil in the school from day one, you know all the staff and the staff know you. I could say to parents 'when your child starts in preschool or Reception, the Year 6 teacher will know them that day, so by the time they get to Year 6, the relationship that they'll have, seven or eight years later, is phenomenal'. I think that is incredibly powerful.

Alongside that, the better and better job we did at providing for our special needs children, but with no funding to match, meant that I was becoming increasingly frustrated. The picture across the whole country is that the level of SEND need is rising. In our school, it had always been incredibly high and was rising further. Our ability to staff that just wasn't being matched by the local authority, who were in a crisis in terms of funding. Our staff desperately wanted to give these children the education that they deserved but it was becoming more and more difficult. I stopped being able to say, hand on heart, that we were able to provide a truly outstanding education for all our pupils, and that just didn't sit with me. That was not a place that I could continue to lead from. It was a really hard place to have got to, but when you look at your salary scale and think, if someone could start at the bottom of this scale, at least they'd have five years of money in the budget to use elsewhere. I needed to balance the budget to protect the education of the children and the model just couldn't include me.

Are those problems less of an issue now you lead a bigger school?

I was really lucky that an opportunity came up in another church school quite near to where I lived.

We've got 320 pupils so we're about three times the size. Lots of the challenges are the same but particularly in terms of funding, the difference is phenomenal. We have similar levels of SEND, and needs continue to rise. Whilst I'm still really proud of the support that we give to our SEND children, it's so much easier when there is money to spend. It has become so apparent that there is such inequity in the system. In my current post I have got the budget to be able to put in place the staffing or other things that the children need – in my previous role we were thrilled to end the year with a surplus of one or two hundred pounds. Even though birth rates are falling, and we are unlikely to be full this September or next, our budget can cope – in my previous role, that would have been catastrophic; there was nothing left to cut.

In my new role, the ability to do what needs to be done to meet the needs of our pupils has reignited my love of the job – this is what the job should be. Since I started at my new school, we've welcomed a number of children with very high levels of need, so we have brought in extra staff. The pupils brought with them some level of funding which doesn't completely cover the provision we have put in place, but actually, as a school, we can cover it. It's that ability to not to have to put more unreasonable demands on staff which makes the difference. If you can't put in an additional teaching support system, it either means you're stretching thinner, you are expecting even more of the teaching assistants you've got, or you're putting work on class teachers who are already trying to juggle and manage so much. It just feels like now I have the ability to make the right decisions in the interest of the school, which means I'm not putting unrealistic expectations on colleagues for them to be able to continue to do their job and ensure our children flourish and do well. I'm not saying that small schools can't provide a great education for all their pupils and be completely and successfully inclusive, they 100% can. But if we don't deal with the funding issues, that is likely to become less and less of a reality and that is so sad. Honestly, I am a little bit heartbroken that I've had to step out of the way. I know that small schools can do phenomenal things for their children.

What is it about small schools that can make them so effective in supporting pupils' particular needs and are you trying to replicate that in your new role?

I think what works well is that setting culture and setting ethos in a small school is quick. You have got a handful of staff who you sit down and talk with. You can spot things that aren't working quickly and talk together about what we think we need to do. Literally the following day, you can make the change and everyone's on board. Everyone's looking out for those children who might be finding things harder for different reasons and there was an absolute culture where we sweated the small things that come up. If something wasn't right, we nipped it in the bud, we stepped in straightaway, and everyone stepped in. So, there wasn't a sense of 'that's their problem'. Nothing was ever one person's problem. Everything was always 'our' problem. We all took collective responsibility. The children saw that and knew that too. Part of the joy of mixed ages is you've always got an older year group who show you the ropes and take the responsibility. If someone is doing something that they know is not acceptable, they were shown with love how that doesn't work here, that isn't the way that we behave.

In a bigger school, developing ethos and culture takes longer. The more staff you've got, the more time it takes to bring people on board with different ways of managing behaviour and developing relationships and that kind of thing. I'm trying to bring in that consistency, but very much in a way that says, 'we're not going to shout at children, we're not just going to tell them what they're doing wrong, we're all going to love these children and we're going to learn to build that alongside each other'. So, it's trying to take the heart of what was so special about my first school and develop that in my current school. We've made some steps to get there but it's going to take probably at least another full year, really, to get to where I want us to be. I do know that we can get there 100%, because I've got teachers who are amazing and love what they do and are passionate about what they're doing. Another big part of our culture work is that we're revising our vision. I want our vision and values to be central to everything we do and it's important that everyone's on board and everyone's really clear. You can't rush things like this, especially if you want to bring everyone with you to feel part of that.

In terms of your leadership style, is there anything you have had to purposefully change as you have moved to a bigger school?

When I knew I was moving to a bigger school I was excited about having the opportunity to delegate again and I definitely underestimated how much I needed to stop it just being me who did all of the work. As head of a small school, you might identify a problem and might aim to delegate that but then you are the one that ends up dealing with it. Now there is the potential for a more collaborative approach because there are more people but equally there is more of a definition between what people see as their role or not their role. In a small school, everyone gets involved with everything. One of the things I hadn't anticipated was that, despite the size of the team, people would not be used to a more collaborative approach and that has been quite a change.

Is there anything that you have learnt from leading a bigger school that you wish you'd known when you started your first role?

I'm not sure there is in terms of the different sizes of the schools but when I look back, I realise how naive I was as a brand-new head. I'm currently completing the NPQEL (National Professional Qualification for Executive Leadership) and that's been quite eye-opening in terms of understanding how things work in different trusts and local authorities. I have really benefited from the networking aspect of this which would really have helped me when I started my first headship. My first school was part of a trust, and the support that was provided was crucial to my success as a new head. My current school is a local authority school, and that network isn't there, but it's reminded me that I do need to take time to go on courses, remain outward looking and continue to talk to people even when I find it hard to invest in myself. Being a headteacher is a joyful job and whatever size of school you might be thinking about leading I would say go for it. Don't always listen to negativity. Is it hard? Yes. Is it exhausting? Yes, but I absolutely love it.

EMPOWERING SMALL SCHOOLS: TRUST-WIDE SUPPORT AND COLLABORATION

A conversation with Dave Ellison-Lee

Dave is the interim CEO of Rise MAT, a 26-school trust in the East Midlands, having previously been the trust's Director of Education and Deputy CEO. Prior to joining Rise, he was an executive principal and school improvement partner for another large MAT, serving the East London area. He has led and supported primary, all-through, and secondary schools, predominantly working in challenging, inner-city areas, and with schools ranging in size from 30 to more than 1500 pupils.

Can you tell us about your current role and the schools which make up your trust?

My current role is interim CEO and, previously, director of education for Rise Multi Academy Trust. We are a group of schools that spans three different local authorities – primarily Leicestershire, with a couple of schools in Derbyshire and one in the city of Leicester. We've got 26 schools, 13 of which are below one form of entry. Our smallest school has got 31 pupils and we range from that to around 600 on roll. I have responsibility for school performance and for overseeing every facet of how the schools run. I don't have a small schools background originally. Prior to this role, I predominantly worked in two- to four-form entry schools in cities, and the variety is what actually drew me to this role. We have urban schools that are quite large down to very rural village schools with complex class structures. For me, having never worked in that environment, it was a challenge and something I was keen to engage with. We've got some people within the trust who are really passionate about small schools, and our Board are totally committed to them as well. We are keen to be a home for small schools and a place where they can flourish. For the past three years, much of my role has been thinking about how, as the trust, we provide an equitable offer to all our schools and how the things we do align. We align curriculum provision, our teaching and learning approach and all our teachers receive instructional coaching. We also align a lot of what we do in terms of school leadership development.

How do you make that level of alignment work when you have such a range of school sizes and demographics?

With our model of curriculum provision, we've developed what we call our Standard Curriculum. It's an ongoing process and we have currently worked on five subjects. The curriculum is written by our teachers for our pupils, and we have a clear standard of what we expect our pupils to achieve. This is fairly simple in a one-form entry or above school, but it also works with mixed year groups. We have developed a rolling programme, which means pupils learn the same content, but then we've had to think really carefully around the progression and the sequencing of that in a two-year program and even more so where we've got even more complex class mixes. We've got some super-skilled teachers in those schools who are able to deliver it.

A large proportion of our curriculum development work was done by colleagues in some of our smallest schools. Our history trust lead works in a school that's got around 50 pupils and so they've got real experience in how our expectations look within a small school context. We are always looking at ways to provide equity in all areas.

How does your aligned teaching and learning framework work across the mix of schools?

In terms of our teaching and learning framework, there is no difference between schools of different sizes. Quality teaching is quality teaching. Where we work really carefully, with our smaller schools, is around capacity. We have teaching heads, some of whom teach three days a week. We're making a commitment as a trust that all of our teachers receive instructional coaching, but the workload for teaching heads is significant – they have to fit all of their leadership work into the times when they are not teaching a class. To support this, we have developed a team of teaching and learning leads. A few years ago, we pooled a percentage of our Pupil Premium funding. We recognised that lots of schools were spending the majority of their funding on Tier 2 and Tier 3 interventions when we know Tier 1 is where it's likely to have the most impact. We pooled 37% of it which provides for our non-class-based teaching and learning leads who work with our teachers in school. They provide the instructional coaching in a lot of our smaller schools to give additional capacity for school improvement.

Have you adapted any other trust systems to specifically support the context of small schools?

We align expectations around the provision of CPD across the trust. About 50% of CPD sessions across the year are similar to traditional staff meetings. They roughly work out to happen every other week. In addition to this, all our schools come together in geographic clusters and receive teaching and learning training from our teaching and learning leads. This provides the opportunity to learn together and it gets the schools mixing as well. There is always input around pedagogical techniques, a chance to practise and, then a gap task for people to practise in their own classrooms. Everyone works together regardless of the school they come from.

Where we do see some of the issues is in maths in a mixed-age context. In a mixed-age group, particularly in key stage one, we have to split the class and teach maths to the discrete year groups and that can prove challenging. For example, in our schools which have a mixed EYFS, Year One and Year Two class, what we try and do is have the teacher oversee Years 1 and 2, and then Reception maths is predominantly run by a really skilled EYFS practitioner. The teaching practices are exactly the same, it's the organisational approach which is different.

Can you explain how discrete year group teaching might work if there is only one adult in the room?

It's complex and flexibility is required dependant on the needs of the class and what it is being taught. An example might be that Year 2s can work on a retrieval task which consolidates prior learning and that they can access independently. The teacher might set them off and then deliver the input to Year 1, get them moving on to guided practice or independent work, and then return to Year 2 for further teaching. It's the organisation rather than the strategies around delivery which makes the real difference.

Staffing is always an issue, particularly if you've got a high level of additional needs in your class which is the case now more than ever. Then adaption has to be tailored even more widely and that does provide some challenges. We use Sounds-Write for phonics which is a whole year group teaching approach but in a mixed Reception/Year 1 and 2 class, that means three discrete phonics sessions, which obviously has staffing implications. It's all about logistics, and that is something we think about quite a lot because we've got quite a few different class structures.

We've worked hard not to have any classes which span a key stage. When I joined there were a couple of schools that had a Year 1,2,3 class mix, but that was really difficult for curriculum organisation. That said, we always need to look at how we structure the classes within the confines of what the school can afford.

Teaching multiple inputs in one session does have workload implications. How do you mitigate that?

That was definitely one of the key drivers around the curriculum development work. So far, we offer history, geography, science, art and DT (design technologies) and the planning is done. There's a teacher guide for each subject and we have been really explicit in outlining subject knowledge and where each unit fits into the wider curriculum. There are links to what has been taught previously, vocabulary is defined, and there is a breakdown of where this lesson sequence fits in the progression. All the quizzes are ready-prepared for teachers to use. It's a huge workload reduction tool. One of the things that we are looking to do for next year is around aligning PPA, particularly for our small schools so that teachers can work together, discuss and share the load. The aim is to set up a virtual meeting space where there is no obligation, but people are given the opportunity to join the meeting and to share work and planning responsibilities as well as ideas. We have a Central SharePoint for all our curriculum that everyone accesses and if they wish to, teachers can share and pick things up to try and level the workload out.

The other thing we do is share subject leadership across schools even where there's not necessarily shared overall leadership. There is far more benefit in having someone lead one subject really well and become an expert in that subject than having to lead four or five. Again, this is where having developed our own curriculum and having trust subject leads really helps because they know what's being taught when and how it's being done. We have the subject networks, where people share practice. This isn't without its challenges for small schools because it's really hard to cover release time. What we really don't want is people saying, 'I couldn't attend that network because I've got no cover', which is denying them their professional development opportunities.

What impact are current changes in pupil numbers having on your small schools?

Like everyone, we've seen a decline in pupil numbers recently and that can be a challenge where each pupil makes up a larger percentage of your pupil population. We look really carefully around birth rates in local areas which has really helped particularly remote village schools, forward plan effectively. One of our local authorities has a great data tool where you can look at how many people are in your catchment; how many pupils go to school in your catchment and how many pupils come to our schools from out of catchment. It really allows you to pinpoint where our pupils come from.

We employed an independent agency to find out more about parents and potential parents in our schools. What they found was that the majority of parents chose schools based primarily on word of mouth, not Ofsted outcomes, not pupil outcomes – word of mouth. So, we decided we needed to communicate the great things our schools are doing more effectively. Twelve months ago, we took the decision to appoint a marketing and communications officer because we could see some of our pupil numbers dropping over time, which is a particular risk for our small schools in areas where house prices are quite expensive and where many young families can't afford to live. In many of these communities, we've got an ageing population and so we aren't going to draw enough pupils only from the immediate catchment. We recognise that we really have to work hard at getting pupils into those schools.

What strategies have you found to be effective in boosting pupil numbers?

We make links with the local community, local businesses, local people, to just really promote the work that's happening within the schools. There is great stuff happening in a lot of our small schools and we want people to choose to send their pupils there because of what we do. For example, one of our schools excels at sport – it's a real focus of the school. They get brilliant academic outcomes but also, led by the head teacher, have really high aspirations in sports, attend all sorts of events and have pupils representing the local area – we make sure people know about that work. We do things like press releases, making sure that local businesses have flyers; if there's any building work, we work with the developers to build relationships. Some of our schools have had the builders in to share what they do as a company. We develop relationships that work both ways. It's not about just handing out flyers, it's about putting our schools right at the centre of their communities.

It's a piece of work we are taking forward even further in 2025 by looking at how we can make our schools not only integral to the immediate community, but beyond that. To make the schools continue to be viable, we have to look further than our immediate communities. We have to start thinking about looking out of catchment, out of area, to the next village or town along, because then our schools become a matter of choice and people choose us because of what we do.

We also make sure that anyone considering sending their children to our small schools and those in the schools already feel part of something bigger. We work hard to ensure pupils in our small schools benefit from a wide range of personal development opportunities outside their immediate area. An example of this is that once a year pupils come together to join what we call Rise Voices, and they perform songs as a unit. Five or six hundred pupils join together at a venue like Leicester Arena or the Royal Concert Hall in Nottingham. It's a reminder that although you're in a school that's small, you are also part of something bigger.

Have you come across any scenarios where closing a small school is the right thing to do?

We've not come across any yet. We have had pupil numbers drop and we will do anything to keep a school open because, actually, if there's a community to serve, we will do our very best to serve it. I think the fact we've got a school with 31 pupils shows us that we can do it. There has got to be a place for pupils to be educated. With a lot of the small schools being in rural communities, the question would be, where else would they go? I've heard of some schools, although not in our local area, that have amalgamated rather than close and completely not exist.

There is no doubt that it is becoming ever more difficult to make the numbers stack up. For us the rise in SEMH (Social, Emotional and Mental Health) needs has had a big impact. Obviously, we've seen a national increase in SEMH needs but we're not seeing any funding injection into that. This is a big strain on small schools because often small schools are a particular draw for pupils with additional needs because of the smaller environment, fewer pupils, and fewer members of staff that families can really get to know it. When we don't have funding that matches the percentages of pupils with additional needs, there is a tension which means we have to look really carefully at how we provide for those pupils. Sadly, we've not got a magic wand but there are ways to make it work.

You have explained the benefit your small schools get from being in your trust but some schools remain reluctant. Do you have any thoughts on this?

Anecdotally, there definitely seems to be a hesitancy for small schools to join trusts. I think there's a sense they may lose their identity. Schools exist to serve their communities – we don't want to dilute their identity, we want to embrace it. All our schools are different. Where we align, we are aligning on educational aspects that you can't really argue with, because we're implementing best practice rooted in evidence. I think there is some mistrust around academies, but there is also some misinformation. I think sometimes it's not helped by the wider narrative. I would implore anyone to just speak to their local trusts. I know of some trusts that won't take on small schools – they just won't. They are not interested if they can't make it work financially, but there are ways, and I think we have a moral imperative to help where we can.

ASPIRING FOR EXCELLENCE: DESIGNING AMBITIOUS CURRICULA IN SMALL SCHOOLS

A conversation with Alex Pethick

Alex Pethick is a teacher and school leader, with more than 10 years of senior and executive leadership experience in British primary schools. She has experience of teaching both in small rural schools, and in larger inner-city schools. Alex is the director of curriculum for the Knowledge Schools Trust, overseeing curriculum development and enactment in their seven primary schools. In addition to this, Alex is the director of the Primary Knowledge Curriculum, a not-for-profit organisation that offers curriculum materials, support and professional development to thousands of teachers nationally and internationally.

Please could you tell us about your current role and your involvement with small schools?

During my career, I have been fortunate to have been involved with small schools in a variety of ways, firstly as a teacher and a school leader. My first teaching role was in a small school, teaching a mixed Year 1 and 2 class. When I took the job, I had not anticipated how challenging teaching in a mixed-aged class would be. It was certainly a baptism of fire! However, what I learned about both classroom management and adaptive teaching has stood me in good stead throughout my teaching career. In my current role, as director of curriculum at the Knowledge Schools Trust, I lead the Primary Knowledge Curriculum Partnership (PKC). Through our curriculum partnership, I have worked with nearly one hundred small schools to date. In my role, I support these schools with adapting and embedding a well-sequenced, knowledge-rich curriculum in their unique context. A huge part of our work at PKC has been to find out what is working well in schools and disseminate this expertise across our network. We provide advice, support, and professional development to small schools across the country that we hope helps leaders and teachers to make the right decisions for their children. More recently, I became involved in small schools as a parent when my daughter started school in a lovely, small village school, in a mixed-aged class.

What do you consider to be the key elements of a really effective curriculum?

I believe we should never underestimate the power that a rich, ambitious curriculum has in opening up the world to our children. A great curriculum inspires curiosity and ignites a love of learning that lasts a lifetime. That is why it is so important that we carefully consider what we teach our children in our schools.

For me, the first key element of effective curriculum design is *valuing* and *specifying* the knowledge and skills that children will learn across the school in each subject. We need to make those important decisions carefully, understanding that for everything that 'makes the cut' in the curriculum, there are millions of other choices that are left untaught. There are so many wonderful stories, inspirational people, significant pieces of music and art, important concepts, enjoyable sports and so on, that it can be hard to make these decisions. That is why we firstly need to value the knowledge in the curriculum and have a clear rationale for why this has been selected.

The choices we make matter as they form the substance of each child's education. When I began teaching, I believed that '*what*' I taught came second to '*how*' I taught. There were few discussions around what children were going to learn about, apart from in English and Maths. As a teacher, I had complete freedom over what topics to teach but lacked not only the subject expertise and time needed to do this thoughtfully, but also the knowledge that what I chose to teach actually mattered. I once remember teaching a whole week on 'beetroot' after being told by a school advisor to pick a random object and plan a topic around it. While this topic did allow us to appreciate the deliciousness of chocolate beetroot cake, in every other way it was shallow and uninspiring. What we choose to teach our children matters. Our children deserve more than a curriculum cobbled together by odd bits of knowledge, chosen at random, lacking in purpose and direction. That is why in the schools I work with we take these decisions really seriously. We lean on subject experts to help us identify what we should teach and why, and we share this specialist knowledge across our networks to benefit as many children as possible.

The second element we need to consider is *sequencing*. Effective curriculum design is more complex than simply curating a list of knowledge and skills we want our children to learn. We need to consider how these parts add up to the whole and enable children to make connections and build on their knowledge over time.

Some of those elements are particularly challenging in settings with multi-year classes. Can the curriculum be as effective in these schools?

Absolutely! In my experience, capacity is one of the biggest challenges we face in small schools. Effective curriculum work takes a lot of time, and a lot of subject specific expertise. The reality in most small schools is that we have fewer teachers, so we are all wearing many hats. Having secure subject knowledge in all areas of the primary curriculum, and the time to spend on curriculum development, is a luxury that many primary schools do not have. However, as a parent of a child in a mixed-aged class, I hope she has access to a curriculum that is as rich, ambitious, and well-sequenced as she might have if she went to a larger primary school. When we send our children to school, it shouldn't be a postcode lottery. So, the question is, how can we build our capacity to be able to offer an effective curriculum?

One way we can overcome this challenge, and ensure all children have access to an effective curriculum, is to work together. There are approximately 3,600 small schools across the country. The fact that each small school is undertaking the same work, painstakingly curating and sequencing their curriculum to work in a mixed-aged setting, without collaborating to share best practice, is a missed opportunity. We don't need to do it all ourselves. There is absolutely nothing wrong with adopting schemes, sharing materials across schools, and seeking external expertise. However, if we do adopt a scheme or use materials produced elsewhere, we need to think about how this will work in our mixed-aged setting and adapt it where appropriate to meet the needs of our children. At PKC, we have developed a curriculum specifically for mixed-aged classes. Therefore, schools need to spend less time adapting it for a smaller setting and can instead focus on incorporating local elements and thinking about how to bring it to life in the classroom.

Another solution is to work with other schools in similar settings. If you are part of a trust, there may be other schools within the trust that you can collaborate with. Some trusts have subject leaders, or even subject teams, that can support across a number of schools. This is a great way of building capacity and sharing best practice.

If you are not part of a trust, you could look to build a network with other schools locally, or even further afield, to share expertise, curriculum materials and resources. The PKC partnership started out as a Google drive set up by a handful of teachers to share materials and lighten workload. We should never underestimate the power of collaboration.

A lot of small schools have struggled with sequencing their curriculum. Do we need to look at things differently in these schools?

In an ideal world, we would design our curriculum to build year-on-year and ensure that each child follows roughly the same curriculum journey. However, in a school with mixed-aged classes, this often isn't possible, so we do need to look at things a little differently.

At PKC, we have overcome this challenge by designing a curriculum specifically for mixed ages with units that form a two-year cycle. Within the two-year cycle, some units will be taught every other year and others have been specifically designed for mixed ages and are taught every year. This is because within the primary curriculum there is some content that is best suited to a hierarchical sequence of learning. For example, when learning about plants in science, it is important to learn about what plants need to grow first, before learning about how they reproduce. For this example, it would not make sense to teach children about seed dispersal before they learn how a plant grows from a seed. In geography, it is important to learn about aerial views before relief maps. The implications for a mixed-age class therefore, centre around the reality that some children in the class will have learned content in the previous year that others haven't. In our mixed-age units, we make suggestions for scaffolding around the core learning to enable both support for those learning new content and challenge for those with more prior knowledge.

Some content in the primary curriculum works in a more cumulative way; children add to their understanding over time. Although the sequencing of cumulative content is important as it forms prior learning, the exact order in which content is studied can be more flexible. For example, children could learn about Australia before learning about South America, or the other way around. When designing a mixed-age curriculum and considering the sequence of content, it is important to ensure that over time, children learn and remember more, and make connections to existing knowledge.

One of the most challenging scenarios with the curriculum is where the year group mix in each class changes year on year. How do schools tackle this scenario?

This certainly is a challenge, and one I see happening in more and more schools. It can be tempting in this scenario to become more reactive in our curriculum planning, taking each year as it comes. However, in my experience this does not always work out well. I have plotted out two- and three-year cycles with schools, and realised by the second or third year that we need to amend our plan for year one to make the curriculum sequence more effective later on. This is why I always advocate for proactive curriculum design, even if we cannot be sure of the class mixes further ahead.

In my opinion, having a specified curriculum really helps in this scenario. While we cannot control our class mixes, we can be sure that by the time the children leave our schools they all would have learned about x, y and z (just not all in the same order). When I work with schools faced with this scenario, we start with our specified curriculum and then use the information we have available to try and plot out a curriculum sequence for at least the next two years, if not more. We then track each cohort through the sequence and identify where they will build on prior knowledge as well as any possible gaps in learning that will need addressing.

We also need to consider what we do when we have cohorts that are split across different mixes. For example, if our Year 2 cohort is split between a Year 1/2 class and a Year 2/3 class. Our approach is always to ensure that whether the child is in the 1/2 class or 2/3 class, they have the same curriculum offer. However, a curriculum that is appropriate for Year 1 is unlikely to meet the needs of Year 3 pupils. Therefore, we look at how we can plan out units that can work across multiple year groups and be adapted by teachers to ensure the curriculum is effective for all. For example, we could be teaching about plants in science in both classes, but with clear endpoints for Years 1, 2 and 3.

Does teaching the curriculum in mixed-age classes require a change in pedagogy?

I am not sure it requires a change in pedagogy, but it certainly requires adaptive teaching. In general, effective teachers need to know both the curriculum, and the children in the class, very well. The challenge we face in mixed-age classes is the breadth of the curriculum knowledge required, and that the range of children's prior knowledge is wider. This is why teaching in a mixed-aged class can be more challenging.

Effective teachers need to skilfully adapt lessons to meet the needs of the class. In a mixed-aged class, just as in other classes, teachers need to support children with retrieving prior knowledge and making connections. Having a well-sequenced curriculum in place is fundamental in ensuring that all children have the pre-requisite knowledge they need to access new learning. For example, in our curriculum, the children study the Anglo Saxons and the Vikings in Year 3/4. The prior knowledge they need to retrieve at the start of the unit relates to their locational knowledge of both the British Isles and Northern Europe. All children, regardless of whether they are Year 3 or Year 4, will have this knowledge as it is taught to them in Key Stage 1.

Other examples of effective pedagogy include:

- Using explicit teaching and providing clear explanations
- breaking down learning into smaller steps
- using models and scaffolds
- using guided practice.

When I first started teaching in a mixed-aged class it was common practice to differentiate learning. I was told that as my class were mixed, it was expected that I should have at least five different activities planned to ensure I met the needs of all of the children. Luckily, this practice is less common now as this often resulted in lower expectations for some children, widening the gap. While there may be times when children do need a different curriculum offer, and therefore need different tasks, our approach is that for almost all learners we suggest 'one task for all'. This is far more manageable for teachers, and children can be provided with scaffolds to access more challenging tasks, rather than reducing their curriculum offer and putting a cap on their learning.

How can teachers ensure children from multiple-year groups in one class can make progress from such varied starting points?

I believe that the first thing we need to do to ensure progression is make sure we have an ambitious, specified, and well-sequenced curriculum. The curriculum should set out the journey that our children go on to get better in each subject. Through the curriculum, we can make sure that all children have opportunities to retrieve knowledge, make connections and learn more over time. If we don't get this right, it is very hard to ensure children will make progress.

Secondly, we need to ensure that children are actually learning the curriculum. As children in mixed-aged classes are likely to have varied starting points, we need to consider how teachers utilise retrieval practice, break learning down and check for understanding to make sure all children can access the curriculum.

We can review how well children are progressing by checking how well they are learning the curriculum. In our schools, we often do this by asking for feedback from teachers, observing lessons, looking at books, having discussions as part of pupil progress meetings and, most importantly, speaking with the pupils. The information we gather can support us with assessing progress as well as reviewing the impact of the curriculum and agreeing next steps to improve teaching and learning.

In terms of progress and preparation for the next stage of education, do you think there are any particular benefits of learning within a mixed-age class?

Definitely! As I said at the start, I have chosen to send my own child to a small school with mixed-aged classes. I love the community feel of small schools. In a small school, adults know the children and their families really well, which helps with progress as teachers are able to adapt learning to meet the needs of the child. I also found from teaching mixed-aged-classes that the younger children benefitted from learning from the older ones, particularly in regard to independence, expectations of behaviour, and routines. Similarly, the older children thrived on acting as role models.

Furthermore, some of the younger children in my class benefited from having access to more ambitious and challenging tasks as learning was not capped by age as it might have been in a single-year group. Equally, some of the older children really benefited from having learning broken down into smaller steps, additional guided practice, and scaffolds which they may have not had in a single-aged class.

Do you have any last thoughts or pieces of wisdom which we haven't covered above?

The other points I would raise are:

1. Get creative with how you use the space you have available. I have worked with some 'small schools' which have very limited space, whereas others have been small in pupil numbers, but not in terms of the school site. I have seen small schools using every nook and cranny

to be able to teach in smaller groups, especially when teaching more hierarchical content (e.g. in Maths) where children within the same class may require separate teaching.

2. Small schools unfortunately have smaller budgets. Therefore, buying resources, training, etc. can be more challenging in these contexts. My advice would be to always be on the lookout for additional funding, grants and parent contributions, and consider joining up with other schools when purchasing. For example, I worked with three schools who had joined up to purchase training and curriculum resources. As they purchased these together, they got a discount, which meant it worked out more cost-efficient for everyone.

3. Finally, as I mentioned at the start, remember that you are not alone. There are thousands of small schools up and down the country facing similar challenges and overcoming these challenges in innovative and effective ways. Reach out to other small schools, build networks, visit one another, and learn from each other. We all benefit when we share our collective expertise for the good of all children.

SMALL SCHOOLS THROUGH A DIOCESAN LENS: SUPPORT, CHALLENGES, AND OPPORTUNITIES

A conversation with Katie Fitzsimmons

> Katie Fitzsimmons is CEO of Salisbury Diocesan Board of Education and diocesan director of education for the Diocese of Salisbury. Salisbury has 190 schools across all phases, and works closely with the Department for Education, multi-academy trusts and local authorities in support of their work. Katie also chairs the Association of Anglican Directors of Education, a network for all diocesan directors of education across the country, which provides professional and pastoral support, connecting leaders to share good practice and gather feedback. Previously, Katie was director of education for the Diocese of Truro and before that worked as a school improvement advisor, school leader and teacher across Cornwall, Kent, Worcestershire and London.

Please could you tell us about your role and a bit more about the schools you serve?

I'm the diocesan director of education (DDE) in Salisbury Diocese. It's one of those roles which has the same title in each of the country's dioceses, but actually, it can be very different depending on the nature of the landscape that you serve. In essence, my role is about securing, protecting and enabling the Christian foundation of our Church of England schools but, in reality, it goes a lot further than that. It's a system leadership role – engaging with key players within the system, be that local authorities, multi-academy trust partners, the regional schools director, colleagues at the DfE and Ofsted. We hold a huge number of system-wide relationships, but we're also engaged in the operation of our schools day to day whether they are maintained or whether they are part of Academy trusts. We have 190 schools in our Diocese so we have a geographical challenge and challenge of scale but some of the elements of the work we do remain the same, no matter how many schools we are working with.

What percentage of your schools are small schools?

A third of all church schools nationally are small. The definition we use is under 110 pupils on roll. That presents a really specific issue in my national work with the Anglican Association of Directors of Education. We're very aware that there are significant challenges around small schools, particularly around academisation, and as a group of diocesan directors, we are really keen to think about how we ensure that schools within communities that are small and sustainable don't get lost and that people don't overlook them. The picture in the Diocese of Salisbury mirrors the national picture; we have about ninety primary schools which we categorise as small.

A large percentage of the country's small schools are church schools and so fall under the remit of the Diocesan Boards of Education (DBE). What does that mean to the day-to-day life of the school?

A lot of our work is linked to how those schools are governed. Within a church school governing body, we have what are called foundation appointments. Even when schools join an academy trust family, they still have foundation appointments, and that will be the case both at a local level and through the Articles of Association at Trust Board level, and to the members beyond. So, the Diocesan Board have representation at every layer of governance.

With a foundation appointment, the DBE has sometimes undertaken the appointment process, although that is not the case in every diocese. Foundation appointments, by their nature, reflect the Christian foundation of the school. Some dioceses will insist on the appointment being a communicant member of the Anglican faith and others will have a broader definition in terms of ensuring that the Christian ethos of the school is upheld. We hold that space so that the Christian nature of the foundation is reflected in every layer of governance. We also provide training to develop an understanding of what foundation governance means, so that when someone is appointed, they are clear about what is it that we're asking them to do as well as where they can get support as they go along.

The support we provide is one of the most important things that we do. I often wonder if you're a maintained school, particularly if you're a maintained small school, who's looking out for you? When you're a maintained school within the Diocese, you can drop me an email, you can give one of my team a ring, and we might not be able to fix everything but we can help and we will do what we can – we will provide you with some options. But if you are a maintained school, who's doing that for you? That really worries me within the broader system; there will be small schools out there who don't feel like they've got anyone to bat for them or to provide them with the information and support they need.

What do you see as being the particular benefits of either being a pupil, a teacher or a leader in small school?

I think the biggest benefit is around the sense of identity and that is certainly something I think about when reflecting on how a small school education compares to one in a large setting. When I first went to see small schools, I worried that the children would feel that they were very insular, that they lived in their very small bubble, they had contact with very few other children and what would that mean? What would that look like in transition going to a big secondary school for example? What I found, overwhelmingly, was that children who were moving on from our small schools were very confident young people because they had spent their primary school years in a space where they were given responsibility, expected to take part in everything and play a key role in the lives of their school because they had to. They were looking after pupils who were younger than them and developing a sense of responsibility towards others, not just their immediate age group peers. That sense of shared responsibility seems to build a very different and special sort of sense of community and belonging.

As a child in a small setting, you also can be seen more clearly than you can perhaps in a bigger school, there's very little space for any children to get lost. Each pupil is more clearly seen by the teacher, by anyone who's there with them. You can't hide and there's something about that. I think as a teacher it's also about their sense of real close connection and relationships with their children and families. Teachers can really get to know their children, their families and their community setting and context in quite a deep and meaningful way. This enables them to teach to that space, but also spot the gaps in terms of how you then draw pupils out into the places they might not otherwise have seen. As a leader, I think the big positive is that you can feel your impact much more closely. There is so much reward in being able to see the difference you make and sometimes that can feel like it dissipates within a larger setting. As a small school leader, you really are a leader within the community.

There are drawbacks and I often reflect on these with my clergy colleagues because it's a similar thing. Just because they're not wearing their dog collar doesn't mean they're not the vicar. In a small school setting, just because you're not in the classroom doesn't mean you're not the teacher, and you hold that responsibility all the time, particularly if you live in that very close-knit community. That can be challenging, and the really happy small school teachers I know have found a balance with that and discovered how to manage that well. It can also be quite overwhelming and I realised that when I worked with the Five Islands Academy in the Isles of Scilly. It's a really small secondary school with tiny off-island bases of eight, nine or 10 children and the teachers live in the community, so there is no escape - it is an island. You are in that bubble the whole time and so managing that well is something you have to be really comfortable with because it becomes your whole identity; you will always be that teacher.

Do you think there are any other challenges for either the pupils or the teachers working within a small school setting?

I think that the key thing for heads of small schools is that the job of headship isn't actually that different in a small school of 35 than it is in a school of 350. The same jobs need doing. A lot of those jobs will take the same amount of time, regardless of the size of the school, but you're going to be teaching three days a week, as well as having to do all of those things. And I think that there are issues around capacity and workload, particularly if you're a maintained school head in a small setting, that can be difficult to manage well.

Increasingly, the burdens of subject leadership have an impact. So again, in terms of the expectations around preparation for inspection, you hold all of these different roles. When you ask to speak to the head of English, RE, PE or art, you could be talking to the same person who is leading on all these things. If there are only two or three people, they have to do all the jobs. And I think that from a leadership perspective that it is very difficult. As heads, we feel that challenge and that we want to take the burden but how much can you realistically manage? I think in terms of a headteacher leading other staff, working in a small school magnifies and amplifies. If there's just you and one other person teaching in a setting, your relationship with that other person is crucial but where do you insert an air gap? How do you create a space where a chat is a professional conversation, as opposed to something which can feel intensely personal, because you work together every single day, and there is nobody else? I think from a leadership perspective, that can be enormously challenging. It is crucial to seek out good support from people who really understand but again, what does that look like? And where do you go to get it if you're in a maintained setting? I think within academy trusts, we see some of that dissipating, and that's where creative options around leadership, subject leadership and sharing the burden can be really impactful.

As a teacher, mixed-age teaching is an art form. It is the most incredible, impressive piece of practice that you will ever see because it's taking that variety of prior knowledge and of developmental stages and ensuring that those children all get what they need next. It's amazingly effective when it's done well and when the teacher is provided with the resources and the support to do it. I actually think it produces young people who then go on to be enormously successful through the rest of their educational careers, and continue on a positive trajectory because they've been given solid foundations. But mixed-age teaching is difficult to do well and it's not something that is part of initial teacher education. We don't teach teachers how to deliver well, in a mixed-age setting. I think we probably put early career teachers off from applying, because they've had it drummed into them that you do this with this age, and this and this and this, and then suddenly, you're putting four year groups in front of them and saying 'crack on'. It's incredibly challenging. From a family and pupil perspective, there can be some downsides. If you're having problems in a particular school, how do you escape? There's nowhere to go. The personal aspects of school life can become very amplified in that space.

You have talked about the benefits to small schools of working with others, what do you see as the future for small schools that are still working alone?

I think this is a really difficult place for a small school to be at the moment. We're seeing the demographic information coming through around birth rate, and becoming increasingly concerned for our small schools. We're seeing those birth rates drop, as well as demographic shifts. We're seeing people move to where the housing is, and where the work is – it's not in small rural communities. So those small schools become increasingly vulnerable. They've got the double whammy, not only the fact that births are falling but that people with school-aged children aren't living in rural communities. Our message to those schools is that you hold the keys to your destiny. If you want to look towards being part of multi-academy trust, there is a chance – there isn't a guarantee, but it's a chance – that this might offer you a way to retain an educational setting within your community and be part of a family that can actually support you to do that.

There are a number of red flags, perhaps where we have a change of a particularly long-standing head teacher, we know that we've got a dropping birth rate, we know that there are other funding issues at play through the local authority, and we know that there's some financial instability or we've got concerns around sustainability. When those red flags pop up, we know we're in a crisis situation. We've got to try and get ahead of that. We had a school where a number of these things happened at the same time. The parents started thinking that the class structure wasn't going to be effective for their child and so they then took their children out and it ended up in a domino effect. It was really within a matter of weeks that that school was down to seven children and then within another two weeks, it was just one and then it was gone. It can happen quickly and it's devastating because often that will be the last remaining living aspect of a community. Lots of very nice houses, but no pub, no shop – the school was the last thing that had life every day.

Luckily, it's very rare that I find a small school that isn't working with other schools, whether that's formally or informally, and so we're now looking at groups of two or three schools joining trusts together. From a trust perspective, that's great because they can automatically become a hub and work together with some systems and processes in place which will enable them to be sustainable going forward. We are concerned that the local authority funding pressures that we're seeing are increasing, and I think, over the last few months, that's become a real challenge all over the country and is revealing some of the vulnerabilities in places where we hadn't seen them before. Small schools that felt like they were going to be okay because they had quite a good level of support from the local authority, that they were viable and their numbers had been steady, are now starting to feel a bit more precarious.

My biggest concern is that when things go downhill in a small school, it can go very badly very quickly, and once it's gone, it's impossible to get it back. So, we really try to avoid that. But the reality is that, although no one wants to close schools, where we see a falling birth rate and a demographic shift away from rural communities, some of those schools are not going to be viable going forward. I think that is such a sad loss for our rural communities because they essentially become places where people sleep but don't live.

In your experience, are trusts willing to take on small schools?

I've been really encouraged recently to see a bit of a shift in thinking around this. I would completely understand a trust leader having cold feet about taking small schools on from a financial perspective, from a geographical perspective and considering the level of investment that is often required to ensure that they benefit from the trust support, but what I'm hearing from a number of the trusts that we work with is a real willingness to support schools. We have trusts who value community and place so much that although they are aware that a small school may cost them a bit more, they value the education they provide. I think that's so encouraging and a mark of the maturing trust landscape. To be rural costs more - that's the bottom line, but we don't see that reflected in national funding formulas. Trusts have got to be innovative about how they enable those small schools to continue to live within their communities and offer the quality of education those children and young people deserve.

Is there a last piece of wisdom you would like to share?

Education comes in all sorts of shapes and sizes and can be done incredibly well in all sorts of ways. It benefits our young people to understand the place that they are from, as well as the world that they are going to live in, and our small schools provide that space for our rural communities. When we start to lose too much of that, we lose a crucial aspect of our sense of identity as a country as a whole. We will have to think differently about resource allocation but we can also benefit from the incredible leaps forward in technology. I think we should be embracing the opportunities, as opposed to feeling fearful of what the change might mean for small schools.

Church school education was predicated on providing an education to all and that's why there are so many of these schools across the country - because there is a commitment to those children. I know many teachers in these schools retain and hold that commitment right at their heart. We do all we can to support them in doing that. Anything and everything we can do, we must, but we must also be pragmatic in the sense that we know that we can't save every rural school. It's a difficult balancing act but then, if you're a teacher in a small school, you know already it is a difficult balancing act.

BELONGING AND JUSTICE: CREATING A VISION FOR SMALL SCHOOLS

A conversation with Kirsty Cooper

> Kirsty Cooper is a teaching head at Grayrigg CE Primary School, a small school in rural Cumbria close to the Lake District town of Kendal. Kirsty describes headship as an accident that happened to her, but she has thoroughly enjoyed leading the school from inadequate to good with numbers increasing from below 20 to over 90 since she took the lead. The school curriculum was developed with her team, to use and celebrate its rural environment and closeness to nature. More recently, they have begun to explore what their beautiful, rural setting lacks and how they can ensure that their children have a curriculum that both prepares them for the diversity of the United Kingdom but also enables them to create spaces of belonging wherever they find themselves in the future through understanding and celebrating the whole of humanity.

Please could you tell us about your current role and the school you work in?

I am a headteacher with a 0.5 teaching commitment. In many ways, still being in class is a huge advantage, every decision comes from being on the 'shop floor' and knowing that what I expect of the staff and children is achievable. It is only recently that I have moved from my safe space in Year 5 and 6 into the Year 1 and 2 class for a term, and now the Year 3 and 4 class, that I have begun to see how moving away from a classroom commitment could be beneficial. I'm definitely not suggesting I should never teach – a classroom full of children will always be my happy place, but stepping back has given me the opportunity to move away from focusing on what each class does independently and consider what story we tell our children through our curriculum as they move through school.

Can you explain more about the vision for education for pupils in your school and how it was created?

As a church school, our vision is underpinned by the bible verse John 10:10, 'I have come that they may have life, and have it to the full', with the aim that all children (and adults) are able to flourish and enable others to flourish as they go through life. The vision was updated in 2023: the school has grown immensely, and the previous vision had become mine. It needed to belong to the entire school community.

This vision was developed with four statements:

Ensure every unique child and adult is able to flourish by...

- Inspiring them all to reach further than they ever thought they could in all they do academically and personally.
- Inspiring them all to look beyond what they already know, encouraging children to have confidence to explore beyond their own experiences.
- Inspiring them all to be confident to lead, having the confidence and courage to be the change and know that, 'what just-is, is not always justice'.
- Ensuring we have created a place of true belonging so everyone's physical and emotional needs are met and all can flourish.

In addition to this, we updated the school values which underpin this vision with belonging and justice:

The dream is for our school to be a place where people can be their true authentic self. As a value, belonging goes beyond Grayrigg:

- We want them to know and be able to bring their true authentic selves into school every day.
- We want Grayrigg to be a place where they can come back if they ever face the feeling of not belonging.
- We hope the children will create spaces of belonging wherever they find themselves in the future.
- We hope they will shape a world that is a place of belonging for all humanity.

It was this final point that led us to the second value, justice. We aim to provide experiences and a curriculum that enable the children to shape a better future, whether this is for the beautiful earth we are destroying, understanding the connection of being part of a whole human family, the understanding of *ubuntu* (one of our favourite words, meaning 'humanity or fellow feeling') or understanding the need to challenge injustice, knowing that, 'What just-is, isn't always justice!' Our children can all be humble and courageous advocates.

How do you think being a small school specifically supports the realisation of this vision?

A small school is a special place, where teachers have an intrinsic knowledge of every family. Even as a senior leader, you know the needs of every individual and know how to greet each child, how to stop and help them or what to ask them about to make sure they know they are seen. Creating a space of belonging for those in a small school is rarely a challenge when you know every individual. There are benefits when each year group is small, nobody ever gets left behind. We rarely win a sporting tournament, but every child gets to participate. When they excel, they learn to support and develop others. Every child has the opportunity to lead from the front, but also to lift each other up and be lifted when needed. Children learn to support and understand each other as they mix with people they may not naturally gravitate towards in a larger setting.

You have chosen belonging for all as a key driver of school life at Grayrigg, what does this look like in practice?

In some ways this is a strength of the school. Our reputation for belonging has led to lots of inward movement, from those who struggle in larger schools, to those children who have specific SEND, who need a place to be truly valued and loved. I recently asked a member of staff what it is that makes our school special, and her answer was simple and took me by surprise: 'love'. One simple word but it's true. All children need to feel that sense of belonging beyond having their needs met; they need to feel valued and loved, which I genuinely believe, is something we are good at.

Through creating a place of belonging, we can help children reach further than they thought they could. We had to consider, however, that maybe we weren't helping them to look beyond what they know within our small school community. We live in a county that is 97.6% white, on the edge of a town that had its first pride celebration as late as 2023. In response to this, we created a Belonging Policy which is central to our school: there is a shared understanding of the terms belonging and justice. There is a commitment from all staff to learn and seek to ensure that our school is a place of belonging, and that our children have the experience and opportunities to take that beyond our school and their time in primary education.

What advice would you give leaders in other small schools who are looking to develop a personal development curriculum which builds on the strengths of being a small school whilst preparing pupils for life as global citizens?

Every school is different, but my advice is to use three questions:

1. **Who is in the room?** The same question for all schools to ensure those who are in your school feel valued and represented.
2. **Who is not in the room?** This may be an issue for many smaller rural schools. It is definitely an issue for us, so we started exploring our art curriculum, which is no longer full of dead white European men: it now includes artists of different heritage, gender identity, sexuality, neurodiversity and disability. As a result of this, our art curriculum is more vibrant and exciting.
3. **Who might be in the room?** We had never considered that maybe Cumbria had a richer, more diverse history than we knew. When covering the Romans, we discovered that Burgh by Sands, a small Cumbrian village, was home to a Black African Roman settlement, and that in Carlisle, our county city, there is currently an archaeological dig of a Roman bath which has links to Septimus Severus (a Black Roman emperor).

In EYFS and KS1, we also considered how we can connect with diversity in the local area and decided to explore intergenerational work. The plan was to bring in older people to share their skills; unlike parents who are so often time poor, we hoped our older generations could potentially have more time available. After researching the benefits of intergenerational work, we visited the Nursery in Belong Chester, where generations are brought 'together to increase social connectedness and enhance wellbeing'.[1] This changed our direction slightly, as we realised that the relationship needed to be of benefit to both the younger and older people. We created intergenerational champions in EYFS, who come and spend time in play with the children, and give feedback to us about what they enjoy, dislike or would like to develop. In KS1, we host half-termly Grandfriends day: the children's grandparents are invited in for the afternoon to play with the children (and be big kids for the

---

1   The Nursery in Belong: https://www.nurseryinbelong.org.uk/

day). During the session, they are able to have a break for tea and biscuits with a group of children, when they can share their photos or items from their life linked to a suggested theme. Next year, we will extend this to include members of our local community who may not have family close by. This is a far more inspiring way of covering the 'change within living memory' element of the KS1 History Curriculum.

In addition to this, we have explored the use of texts and discovered books by Gypsy-Roma author Richard O'Neill, who we invited in for a day of storytelling, which we plan (with funding from the PTA) to make an annual and intergenerational event. This has local links, as Appleby Fair, one of the biggest events in the gypsy and traveller calendar, is in Cumbria. Through Richard's books and storytelling, it has been amazing to celebrate a community that so often suffers discrimination.

Do you see any drawbacks to being a small school and how do you overcome these challenges?

The lack of diversity and lack of museums that celebrate different cultures was something we thought we may never overcome until we decided to explore Windrush in KS1, linking it to the birth of the NHS. This felt incredibly relevant in a post-COVID World!

We came across a short program available free on BBC Teach about the wonderful Alison Bennison who came to Britain from Barbados as part of the Windrush generation to work as a nurse.[2] Through research, we discovered that her granddaughter actually lives in Cumbria and more excitingly, works at a museum and was able to bring her grandma's things into school to share with the children. Through this work in KS1, one of our older children worked out dates, and discovered that she herself was a Windrush descendent. We were able to introduce her to other Windrush descendants through an amazing organisation, Anti-Racist Cumbria. A topic we thought would increase the representation beyond our school community actually had really close connections within our community. When we visited London with the Year 5 and 6 the following September, we went to see the Windrush monument at Waterloo Station, where our two Windrush descendants stood for a photo, proud to be the descendants of those who moved thousands of miles and made the NHS possible, and with a very profound sense of how important the NHS has been over the past few years. This photo will now be part of our artefacts linked to Windrush. We have met many local Windrush

---

2 https://www.bbc.co.uk/teach/class-clips-video/history-ks2-black-british-stories-alison-bennison/zs9cbqt

descendants and cannot wait to revisit this topic every two years, reaching out as this exciting and diverse part of our British history is on our doorstep. We just needed to take time to look for it.

Can you tell us about some of the pupil leadership opportunities you offer to your pupils and the impact these have?

Pupil voice has always been strong at Grayrigg, but how do you include their voice when we want children to look beyond their own experiences or what they know? When I was at school, we learned about Christopher Columbus as a great hero explorer, but nobody had told me about the horrors of what he did when he 'discovered' a 'new' land. We often put too much faith in what we are taught or what is published or shared. We wanted to prepare our children to do their own research, cross referencing, fact checking – something they will undoubtedly need for the future.

In Year 5 and 6, we introduced a joint pupil-teacher history research project where our findings amazed the children and the adults. I have to admit that, on paper, this did not look like the most exciting project, but I quickly realised how irresistible this learning became when I found myself offering to give up my precious leadership days to join the visits and learning. The children began by exploring what our locality is famous for and, like many children, they were immediately drawn to food. We invited a local baker (known for her celebration of traditional produce) to bake with the children, making Westmorland pepper cake, and also talking about Grasmere Gingerbread and the Cumberland sausage. All our local produce includes spices which would not grow in the Cumbrian climate (a bit like Yorkshire tea that doesn't grow in Yorkshire). The children were able to connect that this meant we must have traded internationally. We spent a day exploring this: first at the archives and local history section of our local library. The children and teachers researched and discovered that Kendal (our local town) was famous for two things: Kendal Green (a cloth made from sheep's wool) and Kendal Brown (tobacco) which again does not grow locally. We explored the streets of Kendal finding lots of evidence to support our research into Kendal Green and Kendal Brown. The children quickly made the connection that Kendal is not a coastal town so asked, 'Where did we export the cloth and import tobacco?' We discovered that the local port was Whitehaven, so a bit more research and a trip to Whitehaven (on the greyest Cumbrian day) uncovered some unknown secrets of past wealth. Exploring the streets and historical archive documents, we discovered that Whitehaven grew from a small fishing port with a population of 250 to a wealthy trading port with a population of 13,000. We saw beautiful buildings that in their glory days had belonged to very wealthy merchants. We discovered that George Washington's grandmother is buried in Whitehaven, and that one of the first ever banks in the UK was opened in Whitehaven by a wealthy merchant family named Hartley. The children had more questions:

- Why did Whitehaven grow so much between 1630 and 1833?
- How did local merchants make so much money that they needed to open the very first bank in the country?
- Why are there so many connections with America?

With these question in mind, we visited the harbour where there are plaques to remember the exports and imports of Whitehaven's most prosperous years: exports included local pottery, coal (from mines under the sea) and fabric (Kendal Green); imports included sugar, rum and tobacco (Kendal Brown). The children were able to use the plaques to establish where things were traded and that the final side of the trade triangle was the enslavement and trafficking of Black Africans, who were traded as property to the plantations of the Caribbean and America. The children understood the significance of this – no horrific images or photos were required for the children to understand this, and they understood that people made money by enslaving humans as property. We may not be able to change history, but we have to understand and own it to make a better future. We may not be a city school in Liverpool, Bristol or London with museums on our doorstep, but this history was all accessible with a few local visits and accessing the local archives.

As with many small schools, we were a little nervous about where to go with this in the future with a two-year rolling plan. Fortunately, more research completed by the Year 5 and 6 teacher, revealed that Thomas Kent was brought to the UK as an enslaved person via Whitehaven, whose son later became the first Black police officer in the UK. PC John Kent served in the Cumbria Constabulary – we can't wait to explore his story next year.

The learning has been powerful because it is linked to where we come from, and we learnt about it together. We discovered that one of the wealthy merchant families from Whitehaven actually once owned the land our school is built on. This really brought history to life for the children, some of it was exciting, some of it was horrible but history is something we can learn from and must be honest and real.

Are there any other insights you would like to share with colleagues in small schools which might help them on their own journeys?

I think the biggest learning for us is to not make assumptions about where you are located. Creating a curriculum which reflects the whole of humanity is a huge task but don't see being small or rural as a disadvantage. I would never have imagined that George Washington's grandma was buried here or that one of the first ever banks in the UK was opened in Cumbria – the children loved sharing this information at home. If you consider the impact of the Windrush generations, it may not be obvious in your locality, but those stories won't be as far away as you think. Maybe there was more diversity in your area in Roman times. I grew up in the centre of York with museums on my doorstep, but having taught in rural primary schools for most of my career, I can relate to the frustrations of cost and time when wanting to visit a museum to inspire children's learning. Don't underestimate the hidden stories all around you. We just need to look a little harder. As we move forward, I hope to give staff research days as part of their CPD where they are given a day out of class to do local research into a specific topic or area to find those local connections - there's always more than you expect.

SUPPORTING SMALL SCHOOLS: A TRUST'S ROLE IN SUSTAINING COMMUNITY AND EXCELLENCE

A conversation with Neil Dixon

> Neil Dixon is CEO of the Chester Diocesan Academies Trust, a multi-academy trust currently composed of 14 CofE primary schools in the north-west of England. Before becoming CEO in May 2019, Neil spent three years working for Ofsted as an HMI. Prior to that, Neil spent thirteen years as headteacher of a one-form-entry CofE primary school in Knowsley. During his time there, the school improved from being a school causing concern to being judged as 'outstanding' by Ofsted – becoming one of the first cohort of Teaching Schools and a pathfinder for the School Direct ITT programme. Neil has previously been a member of the Teaching Schools Council and now sits on the National Small Schools Group.

Please could you tell us about the Chester Diocesan Trust and the schools within it?

The trust was set up 10 years ago, in 2014. To begin with it was very much set up as a home for schools in the diocese which were in special measures and so needed support. As the trust has grown its remit has widened and we now support a variety of schools at different stages of their development within the diocese – all of whom want to maintain their Christian distinctiveness. The diocese has about 115 schools in total and it covers a really interesting area. There's a real mixture of schools: much of the area is quite rural, which is why there are a lot of small schools within the diocese. On the other hand, we have Wirral, Stockport, Tameside, Warrington and Halton, which are all more urban areas and the schools tend to be bigger. Cheshire, where our trust is based, is a rural county so a lot of the schools are small rural schools. As a trust, there are always going to be small schools coming in our direction, either as sponsored academies or converter academies because they make up such a large part of the Diocese. Of the 14 schools in the trust, we've got five at the moment who have less than 100 on roll, and they are largely rural although the areas they serve are quite different. As a trust, we have a real interest in small schools because we know that there are always going to be smaller schools in our future pipeline and we want to be able to support them as effectively as possible. It's really important that we have a clear picture of how we work with our small schools most effectively. That doesn't mean a set of rules, but more, how you treat them and how you work alongside them to support them the most effectively. A lot of MATs are nervous about taking small schools for largely financial reasons, but I feel we have a moral duty to support them. One of our small schools joined our trust because it was in measures, one joined because it received a 'Requires Improvement' judgment from Ofsted and was really, really struggling, and others chose to join us because of what we do.

Why were the schools struggling? Was their size a factor in this?

Our philosophy as a trust is that we're not top down – we're not corporate. We always say we aim to make the schools the best versions of themselves they can be. We don't have a blueprint and we don't have a set way of doing things. We don't have a set curriculum. We are very hands off in many ways but we see our job very much as individual school improvement rather than some sort of aligned corporate venture. So, our philosophy right from the start is that we need to treat our small schools as very individual – not trying to fit them into a particular model because that doesn't work. All our schools are unique. Every single school will tell you how unique they are. Small schools, in particular, are shaped by people, the environment, the background from which the pupils come and the reasons why the pupils are there. In a small school there are so few staff that each one has a bigger influence on the school's ethos and culture. Recruitment is so important. If you get it wrong, you have some weak teaching or poor leadership, you're struggling with governance, then you can become very vulnerable very quickly. If you have only got three classes, and in one of those classes the teaching is ineffective, then that has an impact on a big percentage of your school and the capacity to support that teacher to improve may also be difficult to find. In many ways, problems can be magnified in small schools.

I can hear your commitment to wanting to support schools in difficult circumstances. Do you think joining a trust is particularly beneficial to small schools?

What we bring is capacity but without imposing things. The one thing that always frightens schools is that they assume joining a MAT will mean that everything will change – from the staffing structure to the curriculum, and even the uniform. We don't change things just to make a school fit a template. But there are often changes that are logical and make sense. One example is how we deploy business managers. It makes sense to align how we do this to a degree across all our schools, but we don't go in with it as a preconceived idea, and it's not necessarily going to happen straight away. We try to make sure that if something like that does happen, it happens naturally. This might not be the best pure business decision – but I'm not a businessman and I don't believe I was appointed just to make business decisions. Because of the background I have in education, my main aim is to support the schools in the diocese educationally, rather than just making them all run as efficiently as possible. The trust has to run as a sensible business. but that's not our primary aim. Curriculum is another area where we bring capacity as a trust. This is a really difficult area for small schools and it's impossible for every small school to have a full range of subject experts. On the other hand, across the trust we've appointed a group of lead teachers who are subject experts in their own subjects. It's great development for them, whatever the size of their own school, to work alongside colleagues in other schools with different challenges, such as mixed-age classes and juggling multiple subject lead roles. In a small school we often find scenarios such as the art coordinator also coordinating maths, history and music which is a ridiculous demand in terms of time and workload. Small schools working together and drawing on the trust's lead teachers makes subject leadership so much easier. Again, one thing we've had to work on with our lead teachers is making sure that they don't impose ideas but instead listen and work alongside colleagues. This is the way we do things in our schools. They've all been trained to coach, so this is the model we use rather than directing. So that's what they're going in with. Not just, 'I can fix this' but very much, 'between us, we can fix this'.

What advice would you give to small schools who are not yet part of a wider group such as a federation or trust?

I feel the most important thing at the moment is that people are proactive about how they want the future of their school to look. The worry is that small schools are going to be left behind. I think the key is schools being proactive, and actually getting out there and looking at all the MATs that are available for them. It may well be that, particularly in church schools, options are limited and that can potentially be tricky – they might mean they have very little choice. It may be that the ideal choice isn't there, because the only choices are those larger, more corporate bodies, but they've got to be willing to look, and if they find a MAT that shares their philosophy and is willing to let them continue to be themselves they should go for it. Small schools have got to be realistic. The right MAT won't take away your school's unique identity.

It is certainly better to move when you're ready to move and have found the right place. There will be schools in five or six years' time, that are left sitting there, and I expect at that point they will be presented with very little choice and won't necessarily end up where they want to be. Don't sit there and wait and either hope to be picked, or be forced into an academy because something goes wrong, because there are better options.

Do you think there is any other long-term choice for stand-alone small schools apart from joining a trust?

When I first joined the trust, we were six schools, and we had a couple of schools where, while there was interest, no one felt any great momentum. The White Paper in many ways didn't change that an awful lot. I think it made a few people look, but 2030 still felt very far away and schools didn't seem to feel any great pressure. Things have been different in the last 12 months or so. We've noticed that the number of schools approaching us and the pace of schools wanting to join the trust has grown massively. I'm sure that, with those schools, it's very much linked to the decline in local authorities' capacity. Schools are finding that they're no longer able to get the support that they need from where they used to get it and schools are beginning to feel vulnerable. What we're noticing is that it's not just weak schools that are feeling vulnerable, it's good schools too. Retaining 'good' is not easy under the current framework and they are very aware that they are sitting on a vulnerable 'good' judgment. The Local Authority might put all their good schools into the 'light touch' school improvement category and the school might only get one visit a year – because that's all the capacity the LA has. Then schools realise that they're not getting the school improvement support they need to keep moving forward and make sure that they stay good.

I think that more and more schools will academise in the coming months and years but that's because they're choosing to be academies. In the past four years we have grown from six to 14 schools, and we've got as many schools again in the pipeline, waiting to join us. So we've submitted a three-year strategic growth plan for those schools to join. And they are a variety of good and outstanding schools – some are larger, some are small – a complete mix. They are saying very much the same thing – that they know now that they no longer have access to the services they need because their local authorities simply can't provide the services they used to.

Do you think it is beneficial to a MAT to have a mixture of small and larger schools together?

It would be very hard to have an all-small schools model because, financially, it would be difficult to put any sort of significant central team together. The benefit of the mix for me is that we can afford a central school improvement team and a central finance and operations team. So, our schools get benefits that they couldn't necessarily get in a MAT made up solely of small schools. The benefit of having a group of small schools is that we're able to get our smaller schools working together. There's almost a cluster group within the trust.

I suppose the other question is, are there any benefits to the big schools of having small schools in the trust? Or is it just, you know, the small schools are a bit of a drain on school improvement and money. I actually think all schools see the benefit of the collaboration that goes on. We're very big on trying to highlight good practice. across our trust and not necessarily from the schools that everyone expects. So one of the first schools to start doing work on curriculum development was one of our small schools which was in special measures. They did some cracking work on their history curriculum: sequencing it across mixed-age classes, and in localising the history curriculum, ensured that it was relevant to their school. We made sure that that work was shared across all the trust. Just because the school where something is working is small, is no reason for it not to work in larger schools as well. The larger schools feel they are learning something from those small schools – it's really important to make sure that they see that there is something there for them.

Do you think there are any particular challenges around recruitment in small schools?

I think recruitment is just tricky across the sector and I think a lot of people who are deputies are looking at headship and thinking they don't really fancy that job. There's a challenge there and then a headship in a small school may come with a big teaching commitment which adds another level of difficulty. Small schools can be the step between a deputy head and a headship in a bigger school but that is quite risky because the headteacher job in a small school in some ways is more complex and likely to involve things such as subject leadership without a team of senior leaders around you. In terms of teachers, we focus on ITT and encourage our schools, especially the small ones, to take students so that if they need to recruit we can recommend new teachers who already have experience of mixed-age classes, the planning involved, etc.

As a CEO of a trust which includes small schools is there any last piece of wisdom you would like to share?

From a personal point of view, I have thoroughly enjoyed working with our small schools, because I do think that they are able to be slightly more creative, agile and do things in different and interesting ways. This is partly because of need but also it helps them to build that unique identity which gives us more points of reference and more things that stand out. I think it's great how they get to know their communities and are central to them. A lot of our small schools support a much higher percentage of children with special needs than our other schools and again, that's one of those things that we embrace because I think for a lot of children, being in that really small nurturing environment is maybe more manageable for them than being at a bigger school. I know there are small schools that offer flexi-school provision, which meets a real need and means that children who perhaps wouldn't attend school at all are getting a great education. I see our small schools as being full of exciting opportunities. I think they add a massive amount to the trust.

INCLUSIVE BY DESIGN: BUILDING SEND EXCELLENCE IN SMALL SCHOOLS

A conversation with Cassie Young

> Cassie Young is inclusion executive lead for Our Community Multi-Academy Trust, which comprises of ten church and community schools across Kent, including a specialist resource provision for children with language disorders. The majority of the schools are small, rural and unique to the communities they serve. Cassie supports leaders, SENCOs and staff teams to improve their inclusive practice and deliver high-quality support for pupils with special educational needs and disabilities. She is also an inclusion lead of education for Kent.

Please could you tell us about your current role, the settings within which you work and your involvement with small schools?

Our trust comprises of small schools (from approximately 40-plus pupils) and mixed-aged cohorts of pupils. I work predominantly on the ground with school teams to support their work with pupils with SEND and other vulnerable groups. This includes running the SENCO network across the trust, resourcing and updating the CPD portal, analysing data, completing seasonal visits, being outward facing and sharing good practice and coordinating peer-to-peer reviews for headteachers and SENCOs. Having led a small school for some years before my current role, I understand the importance of these establishments to both the immediate families and the wider communities that they serve.

Small school settings can be quite different to larger ones, in many ways, in terms of supporting pupils with SEND; do you think there are any notable differences between a large, multiform setting and a small school with mixed-age classes?

Obviously, schools vary in many ways and establishments will approach things in different ways. I think one way in which smaller schools differ is in the depth of relationships and the ability to regularly meet with pupils and their families. This often means that pupils get a more personalised approach, and staff have the opportunity to assess the impact of their needs and adapt at a quicker pace than in other larger settings, which could be managing a much higher number of children over a Key Stage or cohort. Small schools with mixed-aged classes have more flexibility in teaching methods and curriculum delivery, due to the spread of ages and abilities. This is often to the benefit of pupils with SEND, who need a multidisciplinary approach and a more personalised experience to meet their needs. Comparing larger settings and smaller settings I have worked in, I felt a noticeable difference in that the support networks are more tight-knit, with teachers, staff and parents/carers collaborating closely to address the needs of individual children. In larger settings, it felt more challenging to maintain a sense of community, particularly with harder-to-reach families and those that need a higher level of support more regularly.

Smaller school settings tend to have a greater emphasis on creativity and innovation in finding alternative solutions to support pupils with SEND. This can be for multiple reasons, but generally this is due to less access to resources (space for facilities, equipment, or number of support staff) which has had some really positive effects. An example of this is using forest school space to incorporate sensory circuits for identified children or joining up two small cohorts to give adult capacity to intervention sessions.

There are many instances where small schools have successfully supported pupils who have not found the same success in larger settings – why do you think this is the case?

Depending on pupil need, some smaller schools allow for quieter and less busy transitions, as well as having smaller friendship groups with a range of chronological ages. Staff get to know the pupils in a deeper and more nurturing way and therefore, are more equipped at supporting some pupils with SEND. Parents that have made the decision to move their child to a smaller setting have often commented on its more family-like feel for their child, while having greater opportunities to share their concerns face-to-face with teachers and senior leaders. The opportunities for collaborative support networks within the school from across different phases and year groups also ensures that there is a coordinated effort in supporting pupils with SEND, and the sharing of good practice both inside and outside of the classroom. Children are less likely to be 'lost in the crowd' in a small setting, with more opportunities to shine through with unseen talents or the celebration of overcoming challenges.

Do you think there are any particular benefits to pupils working within multi-year classes?

A real strength and uniqueness that mixed-aged classrooms bring, is the children's abilities to act as role models, and for younger pupils in the cohort to gain guidance from this. The learning dynamic can foster a sense of responsibility and leadership, which would tend to happen more in the upper key stages in traditional one-form year groups and larger settings. Younger children in the cohort can benefit from interacting with older peers, who can offer friendship, support and positive relationships. This can add a sense of security and support to pupils with SEND who may have higher levels of anxiety or a feeling of being 'different' from their peers. With a bigger mix of age ranges, abilities and aptitudes, the sense of belonging and inclusion would appear higher.

Teachers and support staff have to adapt their teaching and delivery due to the very nature of the mixed-age classes, and often this becomes one of the real strengths of teachers in smaller schools. The ability to teach, for example, a Year 1/2/3 class is highly skilful, and often ensures that all pupils whatever their attainment level, are catered for through challenge or scaffolding, which is the essence of strong SEND teaching. This also removes the stigma of children working above or below their chronological age, as at many points in the day, children will be working on different objectives or outcomes and this is seen as the norm. This is also reflected in the 'EEF Blog: Five evidence-based strategies to support high-quality teaching for pupils with SEND' (Kirsten Mould, EEF, 2020), which includes flexible grouping as one of its five teaching strategies.

Children also have the ability to develop long-term relationships with their teachers. Some will have the same teacher for 2-3 years, which really benefits pupils who have difficulties with building and maintaining relationships, or with transition and anxiety around change. It also allows the staff to foster trust, communication and a deep understanding of each pupil's strengths, areas for development and next steps, which would take longer with a different teacher and new pupils to learn about.

If you have a teacher for longer than a year, when children are in transition to the next year or next school, they have much more information available about their progress and attainment, which will smooth the transition.

Because of all the things you have described above, parents of pupils with SEND sometimes actively choose to move their children to smaller settings. Do you see any drawbacks to this?

I think there is a common misconception that small schools equals smaller numbers of children per cohort, but this often is not the case, with mixed-aged classes of 30 or more. There is often more space to play and children with difficulties around socialisation or sensory difficulties can benefit from this. Some drawbacks are that often smaller schools become 'magnet schools' for pupils with SEND who are not settling in or feeling supported in a larger setting; the risk of this is that these schools, who already have limited resources and a smaller staffing body, become overwhelmed by the number of pupils who need extra support.

An example of this is that, physically, the buildings and surrounding areas are not always appropriate - many small schools are in older buildings and in rural or remote locations. Therefore, changing a building's structure and accessibility is much more challenging. Some rural locations mean that outreach and outside agencies will not always attend the school and serve the local area without the families travelling further afield for support. This is where school leaders and SENCOs in smaller schools need to be ready to challenge and to find ways to ensure that needs are being met and that children are receiving the support that they are entitled to.

The resources available in small schools are often limited particularly in terms of staffing and physical space, do you have any top tips or creative ways small school colleagues can manage this?

I think time-management and blocking is the key to working in a small school. Ensuring you can prioritise the statutory elements of the job and alongside this, blocking out time to complete paperwork has been a helpful approach. Sometimes it's easy to forget that paperwork takes a lot longer than we imagine, and that is often the most tedious and labour-intensive part of the role, so planning in time for it is vital to keep your sanity!

Small schools offer a diverse experience because you can take on multiple roles and responsibilities. If managed well and supported by others in the school community, this can accelerate your progression into other senior roles and opportunities within education.

Streamlining processes can really help with ensuring you are effective and consistent in establishing routines for work and consistency in expectations. Simplifying documentation and holding meetings with multiple people at the same time can often ensure there is no repetitions of mixed messages in terms of approaches and classroom practices to support pupils with SEND.

The transition from a very small school to a large secondary is a common concern amongst parents of pupils in small schools. In terms of pupils with additional needs, can you suggest how we can make this transition as successful as possible for everyone?

It can indeed be a very daunting experience for parents and children: moving from schools no bigger than two classes to a year group of hundreds is a big change and needs to be managed really carefully, with a mix of compassion, empathy and strategy from both the small school and the secondary setting.

Early preparation in order to share information and support both children and their families is key. Holding transition meetings and workshops to learn about the new school, layout, timetables and managing expectations as a first step has worked well.

Social stories and transition booklets really support this work and have a greater impact when sent home with the family to revisit during the summer break. Some of our schools hold a 'roving reporter' approach, in which pupils with SEND and those identified as vulnerable can have additional visits to the school, accompanied by their supporting adults. This is an opportunity for their peers to ask questions and the group to find out the answers and bring them back to share with their classmates. This builds familiarity for the pupils and also builds collaboration and shared experience for pupils attending the same school. This is also an opportunity for the secondary school staff to get to know the pupils on a one-to-one and smaller group basis.

Building in opportunities for multi school events – writing events, sports events, etc. - can mean children get to know each other from other schools. Some of our small schools attend residential visits, concerts and church services, so that small school pupils can have a wider network and familiarity when they go to the same secondary school.

We know that all staff in small schools carry many responsibilities due to the limited number of staff. This has obvious disadvantages in terms of workload but, having been a head and SENCO of a small school, do you see any advantages to this?

At first, I really struggled working in both roles. It felt like a bit of a 'head and heart' moment. Being a new school leader and making strategic decisions for the whole community, alongside ensuring individual pupils were getting what they needed to succeed and flourish felt hugely overwhelming. In the first few terms, I had decided to split the week down the middle, concentrating on the 'leadership' aspect and then the SENCO role. I quickly realised that this just didn't work, and the school was becoming successful because we didn't separate our responsibilities towards children, instead seeing our community as 'one'. Once this was realised, making decisions at a whole school level to the benefit of all pupils was the norm and made the dual role much more manageable. We implemented many things, like 'dyslexia-friendly' approaches, emotional regulation strategies for all children, quiet transitions to support low arousal and the use of Makaton. The school was deemed 'strikingly inclusive' during an inspection, and it was really nice to see the incredible work from my team being recognised.

Are there any final words you'd like to share about provision for SEND in small schools?

There are so many unique opportunities and experiences that may not happen in larger settings. I think you need to prioritise planned collaboration and networking opportunities, and that takes bravery and confidence. Putting yourself 'out there' and building communication strategies and relationships with both local schools and wider communities and networks is vital when you are a small, sometimes rural or remote school, which can often feel like a bit of an island. SENCOs being part of a knowledgeable, resourceful and supportive group can only be a positive and productive alliance and, in some cases, transformative for inclusive practice.

I think while there may be challenges, small schools have the opportunity to create inclusive and supportive environments for students with SEND by being innovative and challenging the narrative that 'bigger is better'. I think that leading and being the SENCO at a small school, and now supporting small schools through my current role, has been one of the most rewarding and fulfilling things I have ever been part of. I would actively encourage and support anyone thinking of making the leap to smaller schools!

ISLANDS OF LEARNING: TEACHING REMOTE SCHOOL COMMUNITIES

A conversation with Mary Carey

Mary Carey worked as the teacher-in-charge of Herm Island Primary School for 18 years, from 2005 to 2024. With 36 years of teaching experience spanning from EYFS to Secondary education in the UK, including roles as SENCO, Mary faced a baptism of fire in her first small school experience. However, she quickly grew to love the unique strengths of the small school and island setting. Mary has a particular interest in the role of arts and literature in teaching and engaging mixed-age pupils. She holds an MA in the Advanced Teaching of Shakespeare, with a research paper on Outdoor Education and Shakespeare. Mary has studied texts by Oscar Wilde, George Orwell, Charles Dickens, and Jules Verne with EYFS to Year 6 pupils, using drama and philosophy to debate and investigate themes. She is also on education committees for two Shakespeare organisations and serves as a director in the local Guernsey Arts charity. Her favourite question is, 'Why?'

Please can you tell us about your most recent role and your experience working in small schools?

I began my role as teacher-in-charge at Herm Island Primary School in September 2005. My job description was one side of A4 and included details such as making use of the island environment, managing the ordering of resources and liaising with the island community. As the sole teacher with no assistant, I faced immediate challenges. In my first week, one of the EYFS had an 'accident' in the home corner and then a KS2 pupil vomited. It was then I realised, I didn't have a caretaker either. Residents, usually mothers of pupils, were paid by the States of Guernsey, to clean the school. The days were long, starting with early morning boat commutes that could be scarily rough. The island of Herm had two landing places. One was 15-20 minutes from school, whilst the other was 10 minutes. Both involved walking up a steep hill that traversed the island. The school had to store resources from EYFS to Year 6, as transporting resources daily was impracticable. My line manager was the headteacher of a nearby school in Guernsey, and I had to maintain close working relationships with the Education Department and local businesses, as I was the only staff on-site.

The Island of Herm has been described as paradise with its white sands and turquoise seas. It is one mile by half a mile in size and is reached in twenty minutes by a small boat from Guernsey, one of the Channel Islands between England and France. Herm is part of the Bailiwick of Guernsey and owned by Guernsey. After the Second World War, the island was leased to an Englishman called Major Peter Wood, who renovated the derelict buildings and made a home there with his family. Under the conditions of the lease, Herm had to be kept open to the general public of Guernsey and there had to be a regular ferry service. It also mandated educational provision for the children living on Herm, a cause Major Wood championed, believing the island community needed a school. Children have been taught on Herm since the 1930s, with classes held in various cottages.

In 1971, a flat-roofed designated school building (the roof blew off spectacularly in a storm recently, which was a shock to discover one morning!) was built, attached to a resident's cottage, overlooking the main workshop and generator of the island. The school had one teaching room, equipped with a smartboard, whiteboard, laptops and iPads. There was a single toilet and a corridor housing extra resources and coat pegs. Outside, there was a bench, a small semi-circular planting area, and steps leading down to a small outdoor play area. Initially, there was no gate separating the school from the public, and a public telephone box bizarrely stood in the top playground. One of my first tasks was installing a gate, which became easier after the telephone box was decommissioned. I also purchased a hut for the children to shelter from the sun or rain, and a shed to store sports equipment.

A sign warning of free-range children near the school encapsulated the ethos of Herm Island Primary: an outdoor childhood filled with curiosity, exploration, and discovery. Teachers followed the local curriculum but infused it with creativity and outdoor activities, utilising the island environment. Since the 1950s, evening Nativities have been held at the 11th century St. Tugual's Chapel, an event marking the start of Christmas festivities for the island community. It was truly magical to perform in the ancient chapel, where guests, the pianist and I would all stay overnight. When pupil numbers were low, toys and puppets supplemented the nativity cast. The school also performed a highly ambitious summer concert annually. Our last performance was a version of *Romeo and Juliet*, titled 'Four', modelled after the musical *Six*, and featuring songs from *The Greatest Showman*, chosen by the pupils themselves. We ended the concert with 'This is me', a song we thought encapsulated the uniqueness of all small schools.

Herm Island has approximately 60 permanent residents including accountants, administrators, hotel, self-catering and pub managers, maintenance and estate team, building and engineering team, and of course, the leaseholder. Seasonal staff over the summer months at the hotel, bars and kiosks double that number. No family can live on Herm without at least one member being employed by the island. The teacher-in-charge is the only worker not employed by Herm Island but by the States of Guernsey.

The number of students varied over the years, from 12 to just four KS2 pupils, with an average of seven to nine at any time. These pupils spanned EYFS, KS1, and KS2. In recent years, numbers dropped, and children tended to be within a single key stage. Children of residents usually stayed for their entire primary education, forming lifelong friendships. I have attended weddings, 18th birthday parties, and casual meet-ups for coffee with former pupils.

Identifying pupils with additional needs, I was given a few teaching assistant hours. Initially, parents took on the assistant role due to limited boat schedules, making it a resident position. In later years, a qualified support assistant from Guernsey was employed for two full days per week. This meant the younger children could have separate and more intensive sessions, while I concentrated similarly on the older children.

Despite the island's idyllic nature in summer, the long days and rough boat trips during winter posed challenges, especially when sourcing supply teachers. The commute and lack of colleagues could be isolating for some, and the physical demands of the walk up the hill from the harbour when the wind and rain are strong and it is icy cold add to the difficulty. Any extra resources, for cookery for example, would have to be carried up the steep hill to the school in a rucksack or trolley. Most of the supply staff were either retired or with experience of working in special schools where they were used to multi-aged groups. After injuring my back jumping from a rocking boat to the quay with a heavy rucksack too many times, I invested in a shopping pull-along trolley. Unfortunately, I then developed double tennis elbow! I occasionally sought help from workers with quad bikes or trailers, but in peak tourist season, school needs couldn't always be prioritised.

The pupils have fond memories of their unique and diverse education at the school and have continued their secondary education in Guernsey before commencing successful careers, boarding from Monday to Friday.

Sometime around the 1980s, a supply teacher, working for the day in Herm and finding it lonely, suggested that the Herm teacher would benefit from socialising for a day with other teachers. Initially intended to combat isolation, the visits soon included pupils, who would spend one day a week at the larger school, joining their year groups. Despite assumptions that small school pupils might be socially disadvantaged, I found that Herm pupils often displayed higher confidence, resilience, and academic performance compared to their peers in mainstream schools.

As a result of this well-meaning concern, I inherited the Wednesday meeting, attending the Guernsey school, which wasn't the best choice of day educationally as I only had two consecutive teaching days, making longer writing tasks tricky, for example.

Although Herm School had its own logo and school uniform, it was the same colour as the Guernsey school so they didn't feel too conspicuous. I took my PPA in the morning at home where my resources were. I had meetings with local museums, education officers, agencies like CIASS and the school nurse. I also had a weekly check-in meeting with the headteacher of the school, to catch up on new initiatives from the Department, performance management meetings and dates for the term. These included arranging for the headteacher of the Guernsey school to visit Herm for the whole day, twice a term, where we would team teach.

In really rough weather (south westerlies being the worst) sometimes boats were cancelled for days. In this instance, I would consult with the weather forecast and the skippers of the boat and pack clothes and food. After travelling on the only boat sailing for that day, and possibly the next few days, I would walk up the hill, teach for the day and then stay in one of the self-catering cottages for as long as was needed. There seemed to be a gradual increase of cancelled boats due to high winds and rough seas. Last year I spent at least 22 nights in Herm due to the weather. On the odd occasion where I could not get over at all, I would email work across, similar to the pandemic times.

How did you manage the curriculum with such a range of ages in one class?

When I arrived, Guernsey used QCA schemes, and I initially attempted to deliver separate programs for different key stages. Finding this approach unmanageable, I developed a rolling program, aligning themes with the sister school in Guernsey and highlighting covered subjects. This ensured Herm pupils covered the same curriculum content, albeit not in the same order. Numeracy was straightforward, with children working at their own levels on shared topics like shape. Literacy posed more challenges, requiring differentiation in tasks such as phonics, spelling, grammar, and genres of writing. For non-core subjects, the whole class studied together, with objectives differentiated by outcome. Drama and literature introduced through rehearsal-based techniques, proved effective in engaging all pupils.

In 2017, Guernsey introduced The Big Picture Curriculum, prioritising skill acquisition. This approach was ideal for a small school, allowing studies on diverse topics like refugees, slavery, women's history, and the 1960s. Local history and geography were integral to learning, fostering valuable life skills and critical thinking. However, in 2019, Guernsey adopted Ofsted inspections, leading to a shift towards a knowledge-based curriculum with specific subject areas for each year group. This posed challenges for Herm's small school setup. I adapted by following content for a specific year group on a rolling program, maintaining the small school ethos while trying to meet new curriculum demands.

I continued to squeeze in utilising the local environment when I could and in my last term, we studied local seaweed, its history, biology and uses. We formed a 'company' with marketing and finance managers. We sold our products with our designed logo after foraging for seaweed with a local company, making dried seaweed art, seaweed salt and producing stories. Our seaweed crisps were unsuccessful but the salt was a sell-out.

How did you work with the local community?

Much more than just a place of academic learning, the school was a vital part of the island community, with families appreciating the proximity of their children. School events included participation in Britain in Bloom and Floral Guernsey competitions, with the gardener helping design new garden themes annually. The school hosted various visitors, from authors and artists to royalty, including the then Prince Charles and Prince Edward. It was quite intimidating to have the security guards sweep the school before the royal visitors entered.

The children also had the opportunity to hold the Olympic torch during pre-Olympic visits.

The school participated in island life, such as taste-testing new biscuits for the restaurant and lending glitter for the pub's New Year's Eve parties. Residents supported charity cake sales and the children joined the Water Diviner in finding new bore holes for the water supply. The estate manager demonstrated drinking water tests, and the pastry chef taught Christmas cake decoration. The school was a community hub, fostering a strong sense of belonging among residents.

I had great relationships with the neighbouring islands of Sark and Jethou. Sark School visited one year on a pirate day where we were two rival pirate factions, having a water fight as they disembarked at the harbour, later having a jolly picnic on the beach together. Jethou is an extremely small island, inhabited by one owner and one family. We made the short sea journey there to release seals, viewed white pheasants, and had an end of term swim in the owner's pool. The child on Jethou also attended Herm school, commuting the small distance on her father's RIB (Rigid Inflatable Boat).

Are there any logistical challenges of working on a remote island?

The commute could be challenging. It wasn't like catching a bus. There wouldn't be another to catch if you missed it. I tended to arrive at the harbour a full half an hour before sailing, grabbing a coffee from the harbour café and catching up with fishermen and skippers who had become friends over the years. Some had even sailed me across when the main boat was out of action. The main ferry was a small, double-hulled, double-decker craft with a maximum capacity of 250. There was a period where the ferry lost the contract, and in that time and after the pandemic, I travelled on a RIB, a fishing boat, a sailing boat and a tiny eight-seater charter.

The winter was prone to rough and stormy weather when the short journey could seem very long and scary with huge rollercoaster waves. Storms could blow up at any time of the year, interrupting trips and events and even delaying inspectors!

I always thought it was important to have end-of-term trips with treats such as bowling, crazy golf, and other activities that weren't on Herm. We attended matinee theatre performances and every art exhibition we could manage. As we were a small group, we were always treated well and had individual attention from the artists and actors. As we had no gym, our physical education included walking around the island, ball skills and non-stop cricket in the leaseholder's garden. We were also very fortunate to hire a forest school practitioner to build campfires and dens and tents in our Mayqueen woods. It was through this practitioner and while we were reading *Swallows and Amazons*, that we started going to our local sailing school charity in Guernsey. We were lucky enough to have weekly sessions in the first half of the autumn term which recommenced in the summer as long as the weather allowed. Although the session took all morning, travelling over to Guernsey on the first boat and returning on the lunchtime one, the children's resilience, confidence and even language and oracy skills benefitted hugely. By the time they left Herm School, most could sail proficiently, having achieved the first few levels of RYA (Royal Yachting Association) awards. We learned about rocks and tides and the sailing markers between Guernsey and Herm. We saw puffins and dolphins and otherwise inaccessible beaches and caves.

The resources we needed for school could be ordered and either loaded onto the island's cargo ship, for large items of furniture, or on the regular 'ferry' for stationery or smaller items. Items for particular lessons like plants, science equipment or ingredients for cookery (we used to cook in self-catering cottages, but I eventually bought a portable oven and hob), I would have to transport from my home. I did cycle at times but was stopped by the police for having too heavy a rucksack whilst cycling!

One of the main issues for the school was its appalling mobile phone reception and internet connectivity. Herm Island Company had high-speed internet and there were free hotspots around. The school, however, was on a different system, linked to Guernsey. It could be clunky and slow. In the early years, the whole of the island, including the school, would be cut off if a cruise liner happened to anchor in a certain spot between Herm and Guernsey and block the signal!

The mobile phone signal was extremely patchy in school too and I would usually have to go outside the school to make a call. For a whole month and a half in my last year of teaching there, not only the internet, but the landline was inoperable. Every day I had to try to use my mobile phone, struggling to get enough signal to report the pupils' attendance. It was a little unnerving, knowing that I was basically cut off, especially as for a few days in that time I was also stranded over there due to stormy weather. (My employer had issued me with an emergency walkie-talkie linked to the emergency services.) At that time, using PowerPoints, printing and relying on smartboards was impossible and I had to replan a lot of the curriculum content. Luckily, being a small schoolteacher and having to be resourceful and flexible anyway, this wasn't as much of a problem as it could have been.

If I had any pupils with additional needs, it would be challenging to get the agencies to take a day out to assess children in situ in Herm School. Some preferred to assess the children on their Guernsey day, but this was not ideal as it was not their usual place of learning. I had to cater for all sorts of needs and styles of learning by myself. The island's geography prohibited any physical disability, so the needs were educational and emotional rather than physical.

What impact does attending a school like this have on the pupils?

The pupils all seem to have loved coming to the school. There was no busy commute or long boat, car or bus journey. Their parents were very close in case of sickness or emergencies. The school was a necessity when recruiting families to the island, who, understandably, preferred a school they could walk to rather than putting their children on a boat every day to Guernsey. Any visitors to Herm would invariably want to visit the school, so the children have had many first-hand experiences with authors and experts in origami and outdoor education, for example. One year, when studying the Vikings, we were fortunate enough to have a leading outdoor educationalist for the whole day, foraging for plants and shellfish, building a tent on the beach and sitting round a camp fire eating our foraged plants and freshly caught fish.

The children, all living in such proximity to the water and at the mercy of the weather, were very familiar with the Beaufort scale, tides and wind directions. They had a pride and love for their island that was engrained in the school. I found they left as more confident individuals, unafraid to converse with others including adults and with a strong sense of self.

The disadvantages of being in a small island school was that there were too few pupils to have team sports like football and netball. There was no gym and as such, indoor PE and drama had to be in school with the chairs and tables pushed back. If a pupil had an interest or skill in sport or other activities like music or ballet, they couldn't join the sessions in Guernsey in the weekday evenings. Because the last boat back was around 4pm in the winter, they could only take part if these clubs were at the weekend. After-school clubs were feasible with the smaller numbers, but not practical because of the restriction of the return boat times unless the teacher stayed overnight.

What do you think the future holds for schools like this?

I believe, in the current climate and the way the future is very uncertain for everybody, the need for smaller schools has never been so important. They give individual attention and care to pupils, especially wanted with the rise of children with anxieties and school phobia. They act as an extra family or an extended arm of the family unit.

Unfortunately, in the current educational climate of conformity and uniformity, some of these smaller rural schools have a fight to exist in their own right. Looking at the various teachers of Herm School over the years, it took a certain kind of quirkiness, creativity and resourcefulness to be a successful teacher there. I would imagine that is true of most teachers in small schools. The hours were longer and there was no popping anywhere at lunchtime. In fact, there was no popping into school in the holidays either. The commute to school meant that preparing resources, or work on a display, took whole days at the weekends and holidays. But, pausing for breath halfway up the steep Herm hill, I was rewarded by the vista of sea and nature. I never took for granted what a beautiful landscape it was.

These schools are important as they are the heartbeat of the smaller communities. They are as unique and individual as the pupils who attend. Individuality is encouraged and nurtured. Small schools keep families in the area and can produce independent, deep thinking and resourceful learners who are able to think out of the box and problem solve. These skills are very much needed if society is to survive and be successful in the future. We need small schools and society cannot afford to lose them.

SMALL SCHOOLS: A HUB OF CONNECTION, BELONGING, AND COMMUNITY

A conversation with Phil Banks

> Phil Banks is the CEO of a small multi-academy trust in North Cornwall, which incorporates three small schools, one of which only has two classrooms and is soon to merge with a larger MAT, containing a wider mix of large and small schools, including a large number of secondaries. Phil has experience as a school inspector, both domestically and internationally, and has been a headteacher across a number of settings, many of which have been small, rural primaries. He has a particular passion for all that small schools have to offer and feels strongly that the main strengths of these environments are often overlooked by the national agenda.

It is often said that small schools are 'at the heart' of their communities. Is this the case in your experience and what does this look like in practice?

I would hope that all schools are at the heart of their communities, but with small schools this can often be even more the case. In a small community, everything can be magnified. Friendship, conflict, love and loss all have an impact on everyone, and schools can often become the focus of this. Many of these communities have nothing else. Post offices and village shops are gone; often the pub, the church and the village school are the last things tying the community together. As such, they become the focus of attention at times of celebration, and those of need. I remember a colleague once saying to me, if a community can no longer sustain a shop, how can we justify keeping a school open, but what are the alternatives?

The alternative is either a long journey on a bus for a five-year-old, or elective home education (EHE) which, although it does have its advantages, should be a choice, not a necessity, for any child, in any country. I know of a fellow CEO in another MAT keeping a small school of six pupils open because he knows if he closes it, then those parents will choose EHE for their children, which, without direction, will be the end of a whole range of life choices for those children.

But, if there are only six children in a community, how can the school still be 'at the heart?' Walk into any small school and I guarantee that in it, you will find a whole range of people from the community. You will find the retired hearing children read, members of local religious groups leading assemblies, local wildlife groups teaching the children about the nature on their doorsteps, the local football team coach leading some PE sessions, and probably a parent and toddler group for young parents. Whatever we are passionate about, we have an innate desire to pass that on to the next generation, and our schools are, and should be, the vehicles for doing that.

What do you think small schools do particularly well?

I came to the conclusion a while ago that, when attending an interview, you could answer almost any question with the word 'relationships'. How can you improve outcomes for students? Relationships. How can you harness community engagement? Relationships. What is the most significant achievement in your career to date? Relationships. How do you motivate the disengaged? Relationships. How will you improve the quality of teaching? Relationships.

And, what are small schools really, really good at? Relationships. Good relationships are at the heart of everything that a small school can achieve.

If a child passes through your class for not one year, but two, or three, or even four, you can expect to build a deep and mutually understanding relationship. If you layer on top of that the fact that you possibly taught their older siblings, or even their parents (yes, I have reached that age), then teachers can have enormous insight into the context, interests, motivations and life experiences of that child.

What impact does developing such strong relationships have on small schools and their communities?

I read a lot at the moment about high-risk, low-threshold behaviour management strategies and the need for 'respect' in our schools, but this is often never needed in small schools. One of my favourite quotes is from Leo Tolstoy, who said, 'Respect was invented to cover the empty place where love should be'. Small schools are havens of love. A place where pupils connect, feel safe and feel a strong sense of belonging. If you have that, then there is no need to demand respect from anyone.

Belonging seems to be the latest discovery in education. I see my bookshelf filling up with the titles, and that is not surprising. The latest PISA survey data shows us that the sense of belonging in our teenagers is 63% in 2022. That is 12% below the OECD average. This is coupled with being one of the lowest performing countries in terms of life satisfaction. So, why is belonging important? (OECD, 2023)

Baldwin et al. (2020) find belonging to be the foundation for success, enhancing engagement, motivation and academic performance. Lemov et al. (2023) talk about how to build environments that foster a sense of belonging to allow students to thrive and seek the wellbeing of those around them, and Cohen (2022) shows how a strong sense of belonging reduces polarisation, combats racism and enhances health and wellbeing, as well as driving up academic performance.

Small schools specialise in belonging. Students find connection and camaraderie. Not always friendship, and that can be tough; you might not always get on with the other boy in your class, but in my experience, students from small schools stick together when they arrive at secondary. They look out for each other in a way that I don't see with children from larger schools. It is almost like they feel compelled by a sense of togetherness that inspires a kind of family loyalty.

One of our small schools sum this up in their #TeamTeath (St Teath Community Primary School) approach to everything: sports, competitions, galas and festivals. Everyone is a member of Team Teath. Anyone can pull on the jersey and represent the school. Everyone plays their part, everyone tries their hardest and, most importantly, the team wins or loses together.

This is the epitome of community. When a community grows up like this, those ties last well into adulthood. I live in a small school community and envy the locals' recollections of their times at school together and the bonds they forged there. Now, they build each other's houses, fix their roofs, cook their food, serve their drinks and sell their groceries. All finding their little niche in village life, the togetherness of an eternal community. If the school were gone, these connections would be lost, communities would become disparate and the sense of belonging each person has in their village would be dissipated.

You've described how these strong relationships and feelings of belonging extend beyond the school years themselves. Are there any other ways that small schools promote feelings of community?

Another real strength of small schools is the ability to take the whole school on the same school trip. It is hard to explain the impact that has on collective development, but when you all share that sort of experience, whether it is a museum, a theme park or a river, and the learning is brought back into school, interpreted in different ways, the learning is magnified through recounting to each other, or playing and re-enacting at breaktimes. It becomes a collective memory and, as such, a little part of community history.

When I take visitors to our small schools, what they always comment on is the confidence of the students. They talk well and reason maturely. I think this comes from the way they interact with adults on a day-to-day basis. Because there are fewer adults in school as well, you often find that they will be out on break duty, serving dinner, and on the gate in the morning and evening. They spend all of their time in the company of their students and so, in many ways, treat them as friends. Your relationships are not confined to the students in your class, but the whole school is known to you. This approach breeds huge confidence in even the most anxious of pupils. If they know and trust you, they will talk, they will open up about their feelings, and share with you their experiences.

This is what community looks and feels like in small schools. Developing a deep sense of trust and connection, along with a strong sense of pride and confidence in where you are from. I think my Granny would have called it having roots.

Are there any drawbacks to the close-knit community setting of small schools?

Another great question. Of course there are. I said earlier that everything is magnified in a small community, and that means everything. When things are going wrong, it feels like your whole world is going wrong. Having said relationships are a strength, when they are not working for any reason, or people are going through a difficult patch, it can feel all consuming. Imagine as a headteacher, trying to deal with issues around capability with the only other teacher in the school. Imagine trying to do that when you yourself teach for a large proportion of the week! This can be a huge challenge, especially for a less experienced leader. The only way to overcome this is to focus on the value you put on the experiences of the children in your care. You will often have to go through short-term pain, with an eye on the longer-term gains, but this can be exceptionally difficult. This can be mitigated by being part of a wider network of schools, where you can access support, whether that be a Federation, Cooperative or MAT, or the Local Authority. It takes a very strong determined leader to take this on alone, the feelings of isolation can be enormous when you go through a challenging time such as this.

Another challenge lies around the access the community has to you. In one of my first small school roles, I lived in the community that I taught. In fact, even now, I live in the community of one of our MAT schools, so access to you is 24 hours. People know where you live, you often bump into people in the street, or at a village event when they find an urgent need to talk to you. You don't get the same anonymity that you benefit from in a larger setting. This is true of Ofsted too. A small school inspection is very personal. If teaching in Key Stage 1 is weak, that can only be because of one person, or if 'leaders don't have sufficient knowledge of the curriculum'. Again, only one person is seen by the community as the leader.

The other interesting challenge can be dealing with the community perception of good teaching. Quite often I have found that small communities perceive certain teachers to be good because of the way they interact with parents or because they have taught there for a long time. When you as a leader perceive their teaching to be weak and attempt to deal with it, I have seen the backlash of a whole community come out in support.

And so yes, close-knit community settings have their challenges, but when we get it right there, it can feel like the best place in the world to live and work. I remember one of my small schools being described by visiting staff from the local authority as my utopia and, in a way, that is exactly what we had created.

In larger settings, services are often available to support families which might not be accessible to those in small schools, how do you overcome this?

Well, universal services should be available to all, but we know there is a distinct shortage in most areas of key children's services. Some MATs have tried to address this by appointing their own, which, in a way, amplifies the problem for others as this increases the shortage of services accessible to the wider schools' network. For me, we are back to relationships. It is up to the leader of a school to develop relationships beyond the school with services that they access regularly. I have found that what these services really want is to feel a connection with the school. In our schools, I always made sure that visiting services such as the education psychologist, social worker, police or education welfare officer saw much more than the children they had come to work with. I would take them around the school, introduce them to children, talk to them about what we were doing and some of the challenges that we faced. By taking the time to build that relationship, these key workers would go above and beyond in supporting our school. If you were really lucky, these people might already be in your local community. I have had parents who are local doctors or police officers and who have touched base with me almost daily.

The key to success for small schools is networking. Build networks in areas that you need support. We can't house all of the expertise in a small handful of people, so we need outside help, but don't lose sight of the fact that teaching in a small school is an area of expertise in itself. Subject leaders who have never taught multi-age or cross-phase classes can never hold all of the answers to subject success in small schools for example.

Having said that, I would also advocate for getting the most out of the staff that you do have. Allow them to specialise. Invest in them and train them well. Support staff are often looking for an opportunity to develop their skills. Find the right opportunities and they can become expert speech and language therapists, dyslexia champions, intervention leads, pastoral leads or parent support workers. When your staffing is limited, you really have to see the potential in everyone and help them to fulfil it.

Can you give us some examples of how your schools have worked really effectively with families? Was this effective because of the small size of the school or in spite of it?

The only way to support families who find themselves in difficult circumstances is for them to trust the school, and most importantly the headteacher. We are back again to relationships. I don't believe in the executive headteacher model for example, having done it myself. It works well sometimes for holding on to the services of a good headteacher who has aspirations but, in terms of the community, I don't think it is effective. Parents want to see the headteacher every day on the gate. They want to know you are there for them and their children, they want to know that their community is important to you. I think if you try to dilute that, it becomes less effective.

You have to work really hard to develop a sense of trust with all of your parents. That doesn't mean that you shy away from the difficult things, but when you do have to face them, parents will know that it is coming from the right place.

One of the most effective roles that we created was that of the pupil premium coach. We used this funding to help us fund a post for what was essentially an interested adult. Someone who checked in weekly, sometimes daily, with our most vulnerable pupils. Looked at their work, talked to them about their targets and liaised with the family over concerns, but also successes. This individual had very little training, and was funded through a ring-fenced budget line, but was one of the most effective methods we had of raising attainment for this vulnerable group. We have done similar with sport premium funding. Thanks to the core funding method, small schools are a real winner with this budget line. We used the skills of a sport HLTA, already in the school, to provide physical intervention support for some of our lower performing children, which again had a huge impact on them, but also on retaining the services of a real expert in their field.

The way that small schools win in terms of supporting families, is the unique way in which they can develop long and deep relationships with families over the time the children are in the school. Parents who have known a headteacher for seven years or more, or their child's first teacher because their older children went through, or are still in, the same class, are much more likely to go to the school for support when they really need it. I have spoken to parents who need food bank support, or relationship support at home, because they really trust that the school is there for them. You can lose sight of this in a larger school, where the headteacher can feel slightly less accessible, or parents might feel embarrassed to approach them.

Do you have any final insights to share with small school colleagues around working effectively with families?

I am not sure I have mentioned relationships enough. This really is the key to the success of all schools, but small schools will live or die on it. Get the relationships right in all areas, with parents, with children, with the community, with local professional services, with your secondary, with your local primaries, and with the local authority, and your school will thrive.

I encourage all of our primaries to specialise. Become known for something: drama, music, outdoor learning. It is a numbers game in small schools. You need to keep attracting children just to survive, so get the community talking about you in a really positive way. High-profile Christmas productions are always a big hit and they draw the parents, and the wider community, across the threshold. You need families to feel comfortable coming in to the school for low-stakes events, not just parents' evenings, which can feel high stakes, or sometimes even threatening in the minds of some families.

Finally, I would say, keep the children at the heart of every decision you take. It is hard sometimes, especially when I described the way that issues can feel magnified in a small school, or when things seem very personal, but if you keep the child at the centre of the process, you will never go far wrong.

REFERENCES

Baldwin, A., Bunting, B., Daugherty, D., Lewis, L. and Steenbergh, T. (2020). 'Promoting belonging, growth mindset, and resilience to foster student success'. Bloomfield: National Resource Center for The First Year Experience & Students in Transition.

Cohen, G.L. (2022). *Belonging: The Science of Creating Connection and Bridging Divides*. New York, NY: W.W. Norton and Co.

Lemov, D., Lewis, H., Williams, D., Frazier, D. and EBSCOhost. (2023). 'Reconnect: Building school culture for meaning, purpose, and belonging'. Hoboken, NJ: Jossey-Bass.

OECD (2023). *PISA 2022 Results (Volume I): The State of Learning and Equity in Education*, Paris: OECD Publishing. Available from https://doi.org/10.1787/53f23881-en.

SHAPING PRACTICE – ENGAGING WITH RESEARCH IN SMALL SCHOOL SETTINGS

A conversation with Katy Chedzey

> Katy Chedzey is associate director (professional learning and accreditation) at the Chartered College of Teaching where she leads the design and delivery of professional learning, including the prestigious Chartered Teacher Status accreditation.
>
> Katy previously worked as a deputy head in a small Hampshire primary school, with classroom teaching responsibility for a mixed-age Key Stage One class.
>
> Katy is passionate about teacher-driven, contextually-focused, evidence-informed professional development which is not only integral to the work she does at the Chartered College, but which was at the root of her own classroom and leadership practice something she feels was particularly valuable when teaching and leading in a small school.

Small school life is incredibly busy, meaning professional development can be pushed to the bottom of the list. Have you got any suggestions as to how small schools might navigate this?

This is a well-established issue, not only in small schools but across the whole system; we know that building teacher expertise is one of the most powerful things we can do to impact on pupil outcomes, and that this relies on teachers experiencing really high-quality, and meaningful, CPD – yet because there are so many time pressures in schools, CPD (perhaps understandably) ends up lower down the priority list.

While we see this in schools across the country, I think that this issue is potentially exacerbated for small schools for two reasons: firstly, because of the level of expertise it takes to teach in a small school; and secondly, because the solutions available to small schools are going to look different to those adopted by larger schools who are likely to have larger CPD budgets, and more staff to share the workload.

It takes a different type of skill to teach in a small school where we are often navigating mixed-age classes and rolling multi-year curriculum cycles. Our teaching approaches often need to be more flexible: in some lessons we are giving split inputs to different year groups while in others we are giving a combined input but adapting our questions, explanations or scaffolding to ensure sufficient stretch and support, checking and building upon prior knowledge and carefully weaving in opportunities for retrieval where we can. Whilst we could argue that this is the case for any teacher, the breadth required to teach two or more year groups in a single lesson means that rarely can we just pick up a pre-planned lesson template and run with it. Even when the school structure allows for single year group teaching and a one-year cycle, this still often leaves teachers with sole responsibility for delivering the curriculum for an entire year group. This means that teachers in small schools need to be highly skilled at lesson design and adaptive teaching approaches; they need strong knowledge of the curriculum and pedagogy *and* the skill to apply this knowledge flexibly in the classroom, adjusting their approaches on a year-to-year, day-to-day, and often minute-to-minute basis.

Perhaps then, professional development feels like it should be even *more* of a priority for those of us teaching in small schools – so how do we make it work? There's a growing evidence-base around what might work when it comes to building teacher expertise. For example, we hear of lots of schools utilising instructional coaching with teachers working regularly with a coach to improve elements of their practice one step at a time. There is good evidence to suggest that instructional coaching can be really effective, and where schools can create the capacity to roll this out, they often report positive impacts. However, in a small school where there are fewer staff to take on the role of coach, and where release capacity may be limited, instructional coaching might not be a practical option. An alternative solution could be to build *deliberate practice* into the school's CPD programme. Deliberate practice incorporates many of the same features that are considered to make instructional coaching effective, but it perhaps places more of the onus on teachers themselves to drive their development forward. At the Chartered College we support teachers to use a model of deliberate practice that involves:

- Identifying an aspect of their practice to develop (this might be based on an area the whole school is working on, or an aspect that is personal to the individual).
- Building understanding of effective practice (through engaging with research, learning with/from colleagues).
- Distilling what they have learnt into a specific goal (something that is small enough to be actionable, yet challenging enough to be a significant change to practice).
- Engaging in purposeful practice to introduce that change (this might involve planning, trialling and honing an approach over a series of lessons, but could also include practising it by themselves, or with a colleague, in advance of a lesson).
- Reflecting on how it has gone, then refining or setting new goals to hone their approaches further.

Teachers can do this within their own classroom, with no additional release time required. It's about consciously having that really sharp focus for development and then making a deliberate effort to maintain that focus through the work that is happening anyway: planning and teaching lessons.

True deliberate practice also benefits from teachers having the opportunity to receive feedback within the process, though this doesn't have to be from a coach who needs to be released to watch a lesson; it could be as simple as doing a dry-run with a colleague whilst standing at the photocopier, and seeing what they think. It could be that time is created in a weekly CPD meeting to do some deliberate practice in pairs, or for teachers to work together to watch back and discuss recordings they captured of their teaching – this works really well when there is a whole-school focus and staff can see how it's being implemented and adapted in different classrooms, but works just as well when teachers are working on different things, creating an opportunity to share practice across the school.

The Chartered College of Teaching are advocates of evidence-informed practice. Much of the current research into pedagogy and practice has been done in large, often secondary schools with single-age classes. Does this have any relevance to small schools?

At the Chartered College of Teaching, our mission is to empower the teaching profession and we think that research and evidence play an important role in this – as an evidence-informed teacher or leader we can build our knowledge of what *might* be effective, meaning we can make more informed decisions about what to do in our classrooms and schools. However, whenever implementing ideas from research, we need to make sure what we do is contextualised, and this is absolutely key to how we should approach applying ideas from research and evidence in small schools.

I think it's always important to read behind the headlines of research and be mindful about what we take from it. Lots of education research is conducted under very specific circumstances. For example, lots of research looks at maths and reading; lots of the research we hear about is based on studies that have taken place in the US; and while there is a fair amount of research based on studies conducted with primary-aged children, few of these are conducted in small schools! Nonetheless, it doesn't mean that just because an approach was studied in a different type of school that it's not relevant to us, it means that we need to be aware that this is a limitation and apply some caution with what we do with that information.

We always encourage teachers and leaders to take a critical approach and to ask questions of the research findings they engage with. For example, we might ask:

- **Who** were the participants of the study or studies these findings are based on?
- **What** exactly was it that was measured or studied and how did they do it?
- **When** was this research published and who by?
- **Where** can I find other research on this topic (do similar studies have similar findings? If there is conflicting research, what does this say)?
- **Why** might this research be relevant to me/my school/my pupils?

The question of 'why' is one that I would put at the heart of any research engagement as it can really help us to focus on research that is relevant. So rather than trying to consume all the research that is out there, start with a specific purpose in mind. What is the problem we are looking to solve? What challenges do we want to overcome? What are we seeking to develop? Typically, this will be a 'way in' to think about our approach to teaching, but will ultimately be rooted in improving pupil learning. While many schools might be looking for ways to solve similar challenges, those of us working in small schools may have some very specific and unique challenges in mind! That said, looking to research for a solution is often a good starting point.

The important thing to remember is that it's not just about reading the research, it's about what you do with it next. When we adopt a new approach, we have a responsibility to check how well that approach is working. I think here we can move from being consumers of research and start engaging *in* research: gathering qualitative and quantitative data to see if that approach is being effective for *our* pupils in *our* setting. This is something that tends to happen quite informally in schools, but is very important, particularly if you are adapting ideas from research and evidence that comes from a setting that is quite different from your own. It can be helpful to take a more systematic approach to this: for example, 'action research' or 'practitioner inquiry' can be powerful mechanisms for gathering rich insights around our practice. I'd argue they are especially helpful approaches because they create the opportunity for teachers and leaders in small schools to widen the currently limited evidence-base, building a picture of what effective practice looks like in small schools, and feeding this back into the system. After all, it's those who are working in small schools who are best positioned to showcase 'what works'.

Do you have any advice for leaders and teachers in small schools who are struggling to find the time or resources to engage with education research?

Whenever I talk to teachers about research engagement, time and access to research are always the first things that get mentioned! My first piece of advice is to try and integrate research engagement into the things you are already doing anyway. My second piece of advice is to make research engagement a collective (and collaborative) endeavour. So, if you are a leader developing a new feedback policy, take a look at the research and share this with colleagues as part of that development and rollout process. Or, if you are running a staff meeting on using modelling in mathematics, look to research and evidence to inform the content and then weave that into the session. I think the important thing is not to do too much at once because you can't implement *all* of the research into the classroom in one go – and it's the implementation that *really* takes the time – but which makes all the difference in the long run. Instead, perhaps just look at one idea from research at a time; maybe read an article or do some CPD (ideally this would happen naturally as part of the school's CPD programme) and then focus on applying the idea from that research in the classroom, testing it out and seeing how it goes, discussing and reflecting on your experience with colleagues.

I actually think that working in a small school can be a real advantage for this kind of 'collective research engagement' because of the quality of collaboration that can be achieved within a small, tightly-knit staff team. There is perhaps less chance of ideas being misinterpreted, and more opportunities for ad-hoc conversations. Whereas a larger school might need more formal structures in place to facilitate such rich conversations about teaching and learning.

Access to research may be more of an issue, particularly with the diminishing budgets faced by small schools. However, there are some cost-effective options and, importantly, reliable sources of research evidence available that might be worth mentioning. First of all, the Education Endowment Foundation, which publishes lots of freely available summaries, guidance and insights from research, which include practical takeaways and offer a great starting point to then explore further. Second, I would be remiss not to mention the Chartered College of Teaching. We produce a termly journal which is designed to disseminate findings from research in an accessible way; there are research articles, perspective pieces and case studies from schools which together offer practical insights on a range of themes and topics. These are great for sharing and stimulating discussion amongst colleagues. We also have a member site (MyCollege) which gives access to more articles, content, webinars and online courses. Membership of the College is relatively affordable, meaning some schools take out membership for all of their staff, whilst in other schools, a designated member of staff joins us as a representative 'research champion' and we provide support and resources to help them to help their school get the most out of membership.

How does the Chartered College give a voice to teachers and leaders from small schools?

As the professional body for teaching, we are working to empower a knowledgeable and respected teaching profession. We want to raise the status of the profession and are dedicated to bridging the gap between practice and research and equipping teachers with the knowledge and confidence to make the best decisions for their pupils.

Our role as a professional body encompasses a range of activities, from providing members with access to research, running events and online CPD, to publishing research and acting as a voice for our profession to inform policy and practice. We want to make sure that every aspect of our education system is represented in, and gains value from, the work we do.

We actively work with teachers from a range of school types to ensure their voices are heard. Just one example of this is our recent 'Rethinking Curriculum' project. As part of this project, we sought to hear from primary schools across the country about their curricula, including what was working well and some of the challenges they were facing. We used this to help shape a series of materials and resources to highlight effective practice and support primary schools with curriculum development. The materials we developed were co-designed with six pilot schools, two of which were small schools. This ensured that the materials (which are freely available on our website) were relevant to, and representative of, the important work small schools are doing around curriculum. We're committed to continuing to raise awareness of this moving forward.

Our member events and consultations also provide opportunities for those in small schools to be part of bigger conversations, whether that be about showcasing teaching and learning strategies, or engaging in dialogue with policymakers. We really do believe that it's vital everyone's voices be heard.

If you are not yet a member of your professional body, please do think about joining us: https://chartered.college/join

THRIVING TOGETHER: SUPPORTING SEND LEARNERS IN SMALL SCHOOLS

A conversation with Victoria Gascoyne-Cecil

> Victoria Gascoyne-Cecil is headteacher and SENCO at Worlingworth CEVC Primary School in Suffolk. She is also a National Leader in Education. Victoria has taken the school from Special Measures to two consecutive 'Outstanding' judgements, with focus on using research-informed practice to support all learners to succeed. Victoria is passionate about curriculum development and seeking creative ways to engage and encourage all learners.

Please could you tell us about your role and your school?

I'm headteacher of a small school, with 78 children in rural North Suffolk. We are a primary school, with an integral nursery, from ages three to eleven. I've been headteacher for six years and, previous to that, I was head of school at Worlingworth. I was initially seconded to the school because it was in special measures for only two terms, to share high quality primary practice on the journey of school improvement. Eleven years later, I'm still there and I absolutely love it. I am also the DSL and the SENCO - as is the case in all small schools, we wear many hats!

I started my career in a relatively small primary school of 120 children. I have worked in some bigger schools, including a middle school of nearly 600 children, but my heart's always been in small schools. As a member of staff in a smaller environment you get so many opportunities, and you have to be a really close-knit team. There's also so much more scope to be creative with the curriculum – providing great outcomes for children.

How do you structure the classes in your school with 78 pupils?

Currently, we have Nursery and reception combined, as an EYFS unit, then Year 1/2, Year 3/4 and Year 5/6, which is reasonably straightforward in terms of curriculum planning. We have had class combinations, but this is the structure we've had for three years now and we think can continue for the next few. Numbers can fluctuate in small schools, which poses a strategic challenge around funding and staffing. A couple of families of three or four children can have a massive impact on numbers. We have to be flexible with the way we utilise our staff to ensure we can best meet the needs of all our pupils.

How are your classes staffed in terms of teachers and TAs?

We have a teaching job-share in each class and a teaching assistant for additional support. Early Years has a full-time TA and then the other three classes have approximately four days per week TA support, depending on the needs of the pupils. We use our TAs' strengths as much as possible when planning the timetable, while also balancing the consistency of staff. For the most part, interventions are run by the TA based in the class, as this helps children apply their learning back into the classroom. Our TAs are very skilled at running a range of interventions, as well as supporting and scaffolding learning.

The fact that all our teachers job-share brings both benefits and additional challenges (from a leadership perspective). Job-sharing means that we are a slightly larger staff team, enabling us to more effectively share the workload, e.g. subject leadership, safeguarding leads, etc. By having two teachers across a week, our children have contact with a greater number of adults, bringing diversity and a different set of skills to each class. The teachers cover each other's PPA time, and sometimes swap days, if needed, which helps with their own work-life balance and brings some flexibility to their job. Teachers also teach the subjects they feel most confident delivering, improving the quality of teaching and learning across the school.

What is the profile of your school in terms of SEND?

Twenty percent of pupils are currently on the SEND register and 5% of pupils have Education, Health and Care plans (EHCPs). Like all schools, we support children with a broad spectrum of additional needs. The largest cohort of pupils have cognition and learning type profiles, but we also have a significant number of children with speech language and communication needs.

Why do you feel a small school setting such as yours supports children with additional needs particularly well?

It's multifaceted. By having the children in from nursery at three years old, we get to know the children very well. We identify potential needs very early on – early intervention is the most impactful for children because the earlier we can pick up on those needs, the sooner we can put in the support. We build really strong, trusting relationships with parents quickly, which means that we can work effectively together from the outset.

One of the most powerful things that we can offer is that every adult knows every child. We have a bit of a mantra in our school: that every interaction is an intervention. Every member of staff really knows the specific needs and nuances of every child, which means they can adapt how they interact with them on a personal level.

We do a number of activities where the children work in mixed-age groups, from Nursery to Year 6, and because they know and support each other, they are like one big family! On these occasions, staff work with a range of children, which helps build relationships and confidence. If you happen to work with a different set of children, you still know them really well, and so can still give them bespoke support.

Because children are in the same class for two years, lots of the support is continuous as you don't have that break between classes. Interventions that are happening during one academic year can continue as soon as the children return in September, with the same staff the children are comfortable with. Because everything is very predictable and consistent, the children continue on a trajectory of progress rather than dealing with transitions at the end of every year.

You mention that it is hard to put your finger on exactly what it is that makes small schools such as yours particularly successful at supporting varied needs. What does a day in the life of a SEND pupil look like in your school?

Our vision is to 'Cherish All, Achieve Together', which means relationships are key. We can also be flexible in our approach to find the best support for each individual, which evolves as they grow and develop. This starts first thing in the morning and continues throughout the day - whether that's a cheery greeting on the playground, a question about their special interest or just a simple nod of acknowledgement. Pupil voice is vitally important - and children are more confident to share in an environment based on strong relationships! Children come into an environment where they are known, valued and nurtured every day.

As a child with SEND in a small school, you are met each day with a familiar set of adults and children. Children very quickly get to know everybody, which builds their confidence. The building is also compact, so there's no risk of getting lost on the wrong floor or incorrect corridor. As we are a small staff team, we are very consistent in the way we interact with pupils, as we all have the same fundamental approach. Children experience many of the same classroom practices and behaviour management strategies as they move through the school. As there is a smaller group of pupils, SEND pupils get more opportunities to take part in the whole life of the school – whether that's the School Council, or adapted sports events. Smaller classes also mean that pupils are often more confident to speak in front of their peers. Lessons are all scaffolded to support individual needs; smaller numbers of pupils makes this easier for staff to manage.

We know teachers in small schools wear a lot of hats and time is precious. A big aspect of supporting SEND pupils is working with outside agencies and the paperwork involved. How do you go about doing that within a small staff team?

As Headteacher and SENCO, I have an overarching view of the school, the budget and the needs of the children, which is information I use to make better strategic decisions.

We work very collaboratively as a staff team: sharing information and knowledge is embedded into our practice. Informal conversations can highlight emergent needs, meaning that any issues are quickly identified. We can share information across our small team easily and implement things quickly. I work closely with the staff to write referrals – as they are in the classroom with the child, their contributions are crucial and allow for more accurate referrals. By working collaboratively, this also gives the teacher experience of some of the SENCO role, and allows us to nurture and develop them effectively.

Having an outside agency coming in is an opportunity to access some specialist advice and knowledge that perhaps we don't already have in school. My first question is always how can we use that advice and extrapolate something from it? Or, how can we use that advice for the benefit of a wider range of children, or use it to support other children with similar profiles?

Could you explain more about how you work with parents?

As many of our children start in Nursery, we have a few children joining at the start of each term, and we don't have a large intake of new children each September. Consequently, we are only getting to know a few parents at once. We have an open-door policy and aim to be available and visible: our head of school and I are both on the playground every day, greeting everyone on their way into school. We are able to work with parents and children in a way that suits them because they are a relatively small number of individuals. Small class sizes mean that every child is known and regular contact with each parent breeds confidence. It's hard to be invisible in a small school!

We spend a lot of time talking to parents and having meetings; to facilitate the support that they can access themselves, to build their confidence and ability to advocate for their child. We are very rural and we have a really important role in signposting our parents to support they can access outside our immediate rural context. It's really important that parents of a child with really complex needs know that there is external support for them as well.

What impact does learning in a mixed-age class have for pupils with additional needs?

It's really powerful for children with SEND, because they're not just in a class surrounded by children of one age and stage. There are three years between the youngest and oldest in each class and so each child is at a different point of their development journey.

Our teachers are really skilled at moulding the curriculum in a creative way to meet the needs of every child and make sure everyone is making progress. If you're a child with a SEND profile, you may just need some different scaffolding, or a different bit of gap filling from our teachers, to enable you to understand the learning concept. Teachers are already doing this as part of their practice in their mixed-age classes for all of the pupils.

Much of the current research around inclusion discourages the withdrawal of pupils for too many interventions - citing that this isolates pupils and has a negative impact on mental health. Teachers have become very skilled at putting in place reasonable adjustments and scaffolding to make sure everyone gets their needs met. Interventions are still in place, but the focus is on building independence in an inclusive classroom. Currently, with our small class sizes, we are able to provide a high adult/pupil ratio, giving more flexibility around the support we can give. I realise this is not the case in every small school.

Do you find that families choose your school from out of catchment because of the inclusivity of your school and your success in supporting a range of additional needs?

We absolutely do. When I show prospective families around our school, I try and give a balanced view of what we can and can't offer. Parents want their children to go to somewhere where they're going to be understood and nurtured. Our pupils with SEND have great outcomes, which is one of the key strengths in a small school.

We can offer a provision where children are known and valued, lessons will be scaffolded and we will work closely with parents and external agencies to seek bespoke support. But we don't have any Forest School provision, for example. It's about being honest with parents about what we do and don't offer. It's about parents making the best and most informed choice for their child. Small schools are not a deficit model of larger schools. They just offer something slightly different. It is a challenge – we want to be open and inclusive, but at the same time, you can't get parents' hopes up that you can work wonders if the resource is just not there.

You obviously know your children very well and create a very nurturing and inclusive environment. What happens at transition points which can be difficult anyway and particularly so for pupils with additional needs who have become used to your very bespoke setting?

Transition is really strong internally within the school – we take real care to make sure it is as smooth as possible. We have regular "Rainbow Values Days" - which are based on our school values. We put the children in complete mixed-age groups from Nursery to Year 6, and work through activities in a round robin, during which time they interact with every member of staff. This gives the children an opportunity to go to different classrooms and begin to become familiar working with different groups. It means all the children are working with different teachers across the day and the vertical groupings mean all sorts of ages are working together. We also hold collective worship in classrooms, with teachers taking turns in leading worship, which aids transition between classes and key stages. Consistency is also key to this.

In terms of secondary, we enjoy very positive relationships with our high school, which is actually really small as well - around 400 children. I know the SENCO well, as we often work together to support shared families. We meet regularly and we start considering how we will best support the needs of some of the children, some as early as Year 4. We liaise around ongoing need, progress with diagnoses, etc. I can also begin to have those conversations with parents so everyone is clear about what the path ahead looks like.

Children in Years 4, 5 and 6 enjoy opportunities to visit the high school for enrichment days – e.g. a Music Day or a Science Day. Our year groups are around 10 children, and our children usually meet their peers from another primary school on these days, which gives them opportunities to build tentative relationships with others. We usually send a TA on these days to facilitate these friendships, so the children get the most out of them. By the time the children are in Year 6, they are doing additional visits, and if necessary, further visits and support are put in place for particular pupils. Our High School works in a very similar way to us - they are needs-led and seek to support pupils individually.

Based on our practice in primary, the high school also have vertical groupings in their tutor groups. When children start high school, they will be in a form with other pupils from Years 7 to 11, and they are often back in a group with many of their friends from primary.

Pupil voice is important for secondary transition. They often know what they want and what would work for them. It's empowering for them to say, 'I don't think I need that', or 'Yes, I think I really do need that, because I've got these questions I want answered'. With such a small group, we can really listen to everyone, and the child's voice can be heard so clearly, we work with them on that all the way through.

Do you feel pupils can have more voice in small schools?

Absolutely – it's just the nature of our school. Children with SEND are fully integrated and represented in our school - they sit on the School Council, they are collective worship or sports ambassadors. The voices of all our pupils are important, and we seek ways to support our pupils with SEND to take an active role in these groups.

The way our school is structured enables informal conversations (e.g. over lunchtime). You often get far more of an insight into the child's thoughts when they are chatting in this situation. They will often tell you about something that happens in class, or a strategy that worked well. As I said, every interaction is an intervention!

Smaller numbers of pupils mean that we can seek out their thoughts and feelings. Pupils play an active role in writing their one-page profiles, which are updated regularly. Pupils see that these are actively used by staff and are really meaningful documents. This is part of being valued and known.

There's also something about the relationships you can develop between a smaller group of adults and children, and amongst the children themselves. Our children are so supportive of each other. They are used to doing things together in mixed ages and stages across the school. In a sense, they are just incredibly inclusive around each other's strengths or areas that they need support with – they know each other so well.

Do you think there are any challenges for supporting children with SEND in small schools beyond the physical space, which is what we've already talked about?

I've certainly worked in larger schools where maybe you have specialist TAs, for example, who have a particular skill and a particular passion for supporting children with specific needs. We don't have those kind of roles, but our staff upskill themselves in whatever they need, and they become incredibly talented in a huge range of interventions and support. Sometimes I see some of the things we can't offer, and that can be frustrating. But in that kind of scenario, we just try and solve the problem together. None of our staff work in isolation and no one holds all the answers – we constantly draw on our collective wisdom. As I said, physical space can be an issue, but we do the best we can.

You have provided some really interesting insights into your school. Do you think there is anything a larger setting could learn from a setting such as yours in terms of supporting SEND pupils?

One of the things that I've learned by being in a smaller school is that we have to be outward-looking and continually seek out best practice. I get to go out and work with other schools and see what practice they're doing through my system leadership work. This is an active drive to see other practice, magpie ideas, and try and find ways we can improve what we do. It's really instilled in our ethos, because we just know we haven't got all the answers.

Another thing we do really well is make sure our provision is needs-led rather than diagnosis-led. We can't do everything that might be suggested for a group of children with a particular diagnosis. However, we make sure we consider the child's needs and what we can do to most effectively support them. We want everybody and anybody walking into our school to feel like they are supported, cared for and that they belong.

FROM MOORLAND CHALLENGES TO COMMUNITY CONNECTIONS: LEADING A RURAL SMALL SCHOOL

A conversation with Ed Finch

> Ed Finch is a podcast host, writer, education consultant and storyteller. Until July 2023, Ed was headteacher at Chagford Primary School in the heart of the Dartmoor National Park – a small school with 130 pupils on roll. Prior to taking on that headship, Ed had taught in a variety of schools in urban East Oxford as well as overseas. Ed is the co-founder of #BrewEd and the organiser of Oxford Reading Spree. He is passionate about the power of connection and creative collaboration. Ed works with Whole Education to help schools create environments in which pupils thrive and with HeadsUp4HTs leading on the Big Education Conversation.

Please can you tell us about your most recent role and your experience working in small schools?

Until I moved to Devon, at the mid-point of the pandemic, I had worked in much bigger schools. I cut my teaching teeth overseas in Africa and Poland before finding work in UK state schools – first in a big middle school, then in urban primaries in East Oxford.

In Ethiopia, teaching at a high school high up in the Simien Mountains, I had taught classes with as many pupils as were in the whole of the school that I led in Devon.

Chagford Primary is on Dartmoor in an ancient town surrounded by woods and hills – the river Teign rushes past not far from the school. I would often arrive at school first thing in the morning and find the car park full of wild ponies who needed to be shifted along before I could park the car.

Like many rural schools, Chagford Primary serves a very mixed community. There are families who have farmed in the area for generations, incomers and blow-ins; people for whom the countryside is a blessed release from urban life and people for whom life in an isolated town surrounded by moorland has become an inescapable trap.

What attracted you to the role of headteacher in a small school?

I had always hoped to lead a school some day – I used to flippantly say that I had seen enough heads making terrible decisions, I wanted the freedom to make my own. I never mentioned it to anyone but in my head, I knew I wanted to take on a headship before my fiftieth birthday – and I did, by a matter of months!

I moved from Oxford down to the South West to take on a role developing curriculum across the multi-academy trust, but matters developed quickly once I, and the new CEO, were in post and I was asked to take on the leadership at Chagford. Not the usual way into the job! I was pleased though, as Chagford is a beautiful school in a beautiful location and has a community that I knew I could get along with – full of artists, characters and oddballs!

To me this was an offer I couldn't turn down and I am very glad that I took it up.

Having worked in larger schools, what were your initial reflections on taking up this post?

Leading a school is a deeply human business. It's about relationships and connections. In a small school, that becomes doubly and triply true. I could greet every member of staff as they arrived at work each morning, have those quick conversations which give tiny course corrections and shape things day by day. I rarely needed to send internal emails knowing that it would be more authentic, more convenient and more likely to land if I walked a few steps and had a conversation.

The lack of flexibility in staffing struck me quickly. In a two-form entry primary school there are enough human resources that one can usually shift things around to cover gaps; it may not be ideal but you can do it. This just isn't the case in a tightly resourced small school. Through those difficult days after the last lockdown, when we were trying to get back to 'normal', I would dread my phone ringing as I drove into work, knowing that it was likely to be a colleague telling me they needed to isolate and that I would have to try and find staffing from somewhere. More often than not, the only resource I had to draw on was myself. I'm sure that this was happening in bigger schools also, but I do think the margins in a small school made it starker and that they continue to do so.

Very soon after taking on the role, hard decisions had to be made about staffing, and I found myself teaching around fifty percent of the week. This was more than the classroom contact I had had as a deputy head in a big school.

What were the best bits of the role?

Without doubt, the best part of my role was the privilege of being welcomed into the heart of the community at Chagford. At the time of writing, it's a little over a year since I stepped down and I miss some of the children and families terribly.

As headteacher in a small school I could know every child, and most of the parents, by name. I greeted them as they walked onto the site in the morning and said goodbye as they left. I would chat to uncles, aunties, grandparents and community members as I walked through the town. I would take groups of children to sing at events at the church and know that a good many of the congregation had attended the school themselves or had a connection to a child currently on roll.

After the pandemic, events like carol singing under the trees on the playground and bringing the town in for a community fair or to watch the children perform our idiosyncratic version of *A Midsummer Night's Dream* were powerful, not just for the children and their families but for the whole community.

It was easy to take the temperature of the school by taking a walk around. By doing that a couple of times daily and sticking my head into each class I felt I had a good handle on each teacher's strengths and their areas for development. I could get a sense what it was like to be a pupil in each teacher's class very quickly. This could happen more organically than in larger schools I have worked in.

When I stepped down from headship, one of the kindest gifts I was given was a painting by the artist illustrator Sarah McIntyre summing up my time in the role. She has me wearing my ridiculous robes (don't ask), playing guitar and singing my heart out, children all around doing wonderful creative things, surrounded by books and oak leaves, the school cat watching from the margins. Without being too sentimental, if that's the way I'm remembered, then I am very happy indeed. Leading Chagford Primary will remain one of the great pleasures and privileges of my life.

What were the particular challenges?

Leading Chagford Primary certainly brought challenges that I hadn't faced before. A hound from the local hunt running wild in the Forest School area. Daily mountains of dung from Dartmoor ponies in the car park. A lamb breaching the fence and joining in with singing assembly (it was ok – Mrs Rowe swung into 'Old MacDonald' and a confident Year One rugby player tackled it). Not many days passed without a reminder of our rural setting and the lack of an onsite site manager to deal with the 'situations' that arose.

So, when I think about the particular challenges of my time at Chagford, it's not easy to pick out which were associated with the size of the school and which were linked to the rural context. The vast majority of small schools are in rural areas and the issues are certainly linked.

Poverty is very real in the countryside and, for a family, struggling on benefits and without a car, the effects can be magnified immensely. If you can't drive to the nearest supermarket and you're reliant on the local Spar with its lack of choice and its high prices, things can become very precarious very quickly. Add in the ready availability of drugs through county lines networks, and the lack of anything to do, and things can turn nasty.

Teachers and headteachers working in urban areas know how hard it is to access services for young people – in rural areas this is exacerbated by the distance you might have to travel. Let's say you can get an appointment for your young person; that meeting might be a very long way away. Families without cars are further disadvantaged and even those with transport find this understandably challenging.

Recruitment is a challenge for rural schools; young teachers mostly don't want to live in a little village in what seems to be the middle of nowhere and the pool of people who might take roles as teaching assistants, lunchtime supervisors, cleaners and so forth is very limited. Finding skilled people to work with our pupils with special needs was very hard indeed. At times fulfilling the basics of EHCPs seemed impossible.

These problems are more associated with the context of the school than its size. Other issues were associated more directly with the number of children on roll. In bigger schools, there are simply more people around to share roles. I lost count of things that I was nominally in charge of. For example, at my previous school we had been able to employ a homeschool link worker who took much of the workload of the designated safeguarding lead – I quickly learned how much time and emotional burden the role can bring when there's no one else to convene a team around the child or spend the day on the phone to the MASH.

When I compared my role with that of leaders in larger schools, I envied the time they could give to jobs – they seemed to be able to set aside a few hours to work calmly on a policy document or a school improvement plan. I might plan for that, but I knew that I would be nipping in and out to teach phonics, to take a playtime and lunch duty so colleagues could get a break, to help an overwhelmed child to regulate, deal with a parent inquiry, or step in to teach while a teacher dealt with an incident.

This doesn't just mean that small school heads have less time to complete tasks compared to leaders in bigger schools - and, remember, the statutory duties, and associated paperwork, are just the same – it means the time we do have tends to be broken into smaller chunks. Jobs which need a few hours of uninterrupted, deep consideration, get broken up into many little chunks of time. This can be frustrating and burdensome.

A challenge of leadership which is still not sufficiently recognised and discussed is the emotional load and the need for supervision – whether formal or informal. In my previous setting, I had not understood how much support I received from members of the senior leadership team. Those times talking over events and incidents, often coupled with laughter, tea and biscuits, are vital for wellbeing.

In a small setting where you might be your own senior leadership team, there can be very few opportunities to unburden yourself, show vulnerability and regroup. Headship, though a great privilege, can be a very lonely job indeed. I was never a superhero head who couldn't admit a mistake or display vulnerability to colleagues for fear of being 'found out' – nonetheless there were times when I had to hold things close. I was very lucky indeed to have a wonderful pair of heads working locally who took me under their wing and welcomed me to their get togethers, where we could wrestle with documents, figure out a common response to demands, laugh, occasionally cry and generally prop each other up. Without them, I would not have lasted as long as I did.

Why did you choose to step down from headship?

For me, push came to shove when I realised that I was simply not emotionally or physically present for my own child. With no mother and no siblings, and living in a new county, I was the only person in their life who really should have been there for them – and I just wasn't.

I was leaving for work early in the morning before my child was out of bed and returning later than I should – already tired and emotionally drained from the day. There was no moment of crisis but I reflected on my relationship with my own father, who had always felt he had to prioritise work and was not really a presence in my life as I grew up, and I resolved that I had to do better. It wasn't ok to be making sure that I was there to greet pupils at the gate so that they could start their day with reassurance and a familiar face, but not to be there for my own child.

Since giving up the role I have been able to work from home several days a week. I'm there to wake my kid up if need be and to drive them into college when they are running a little late – or when we just fancy a chat or some quiet time sitting together. My earnings have been much reduced and I miss my colleagues and the children but I haven't regretted my decision for a second.

Do you see any way policy makers could address these systemic issues which make small school leadership so complex?

I would love to move back into headship in the future, but I would need to be able to have freedom to create the curriculum that the children deserve and the capacity to work with staff to make sure that curriculum was being delivered as I would want to see it done. I think that I would be able to do that job very well, but it isn't the job I was able to do during my time as a head.

At the time of writing, we have just had an announcement from Ofsted that they are going to looking at adjusting their frameworks for inspection to make them appropriate to the sector. I am hopeful that there will be recognition that subject coordination in small schools, just as an example, looks very different to how it looks in a school with sufficient staff that each subject be led by a dedicated, trained, knowledgeable teacher.

I would like to see serious thought put into what we actually want from our headteachers. If we, as a nation, think we want them to lead on teaching and learning and on the relationship between the school and the community, then we need to ask who we think should be managing budgets, dealing with contractors, filling out health and safety audits, maintaining a record of asbestos, checking the single central record, ensuring website compliance, unblocking the toilet and the other myriad jobs that get between the headteacher and the bit of the job they actually applied for.

Typically, the budget for a small school does not support the position of a school business manager. This means that jobs which would fall to an SBM in a typical two-form entry school end up on the shoulders of a head who is, most likely, already dealing with a teaching load beyond that expected of a head in a larger setting.

Colleagues who have been in the teaching profession for a while might remember the great document telling us what tasks teachers should not be expected to fulfil as they didn't require 'professional judgement'. For a while we knew we shouldn't be expected to file documents, input data, do displays and so forth. Much of that has fallen away as school budgets and staffing have shrunk but it's a useful thought experiment to ask which tasks should be taken from the head's job list.

Just imagine if the regional schools commissioner got involved if they heard that a headteacher was taking on more than a certain percentage of classroom commitment or fulfilling roles which didn't require their professional judgement? Imagine if an Ofsted inspection on leadership and management sought to establish that a head had sufficient time – in unbroken blocks – to achieve the important tasks? A guarantee that a full day a week could be taken off site would be a significant step in this direction, and the new commitment from Ofsted that they will only call on a Monday takes away one of the major factors that has prevented this in the past.

What advice would you give to colleagues seeking their first headship in a small school?

Moving from any middle leader role to headship is a big step. Often bigger than colleagues understand before they make the shift. Leadership of a small school is certainly not an easier way into school leadership. If you've been an assistant or deputy in a full one-form entry or a larger setting you'll find it a big adjustment not to have a full senior leadership team. If you're used to not having a teaching commitment, that will change – just when you're also embarking on one of the steepest learning curves of your professional life. However, if your understanding of school leadership is centred on relationships – with pupils, colleagues, families and the community you serve – then you won't find a richer and more satisfying context than a small school.

Look for the positives and amplify them. Put the negatives into context and don't let them define you. Make connections with people who can support you. Be as selfish as you need to be when it comes to your own wellbeing. As Tim Brighouse liked to say, 'Look for the gaps in the hedges'!

TEACHING IN MIXED-AGE INFANT CLASSES: CHALLENGES, STRATEGIES, AND REWARDS

A conversation with Jacqueline Bone

> Jacqueline Bone is a teacher at FitzHerbert CofE Primary School, which is one of four village schools in a federation of similar schools in Derbyshire. She has taught here since very early in her career and is a huge champion of small schools with all their joys and challenges! Jacqueline's interests include keeping up with the theories surrounding early reading and teaching phonics, as well as being PSHE and RSE Lead across the federation.

Please could you tell us about your role and a bit more about your school?

I have been teaching in my current setting, a small village school in Derbyshire, for the past six years (having qualified eight years ago). At the moment, I teach four days a week in the infant class, which consists of Reception, Year 1 and Year 2, although I did teach the juniors as well to start with. I love teaching this age group and seeing the children flourish as they settle into their learning and the wider school community. The difference between the child just starting out in Reception and the same one at the end of Year 2 is incredible, which reflects the vast progress they have made. Of course, having four, five, six and seven year olds in the same class altogether, brings its own particular challenges and delights.

The class structure of our school changes between having two or three classes, depending on numbers. For example next year, we will have a Reception/Year 1/Year 2 class, then a Year 3/Year 4 class and a Year 5/Year 6 class in the mornings, which will become one class in the afternoons. We offer wrap around care and are very lucky to have our own school cook, who goes above and beyond to accommodate everyone. Establishing good relationships with parents is essential in any setting, but especially in a school like ours: as one of their children leave the infants, another one could be starting in Reception – I may be one of their children's teachers for six or more years! In the second half of the summer term, we have a Sports Week where the children get to participate in sports they may not have tried before, such as wheelchair basketball or zorbing, as well as attending sports events throughout the year. I think that during their time here, the children feel part of a wider community, as we form links with the village church and people from the village by inviting them in for coffee mornings and to be part of the audience for nativities and summer plays.

How do you organise your class to ensure all children receive their full curriculum entitlement?

With difficulty! Because the infant class consists of two curriculums, it can be tricky to make sure that all the children get what they need. Day-to-day, there is me and a teaching assistant in the infants. The reception children have their own bespoke curriculum to meet the requirements of the EYFS Framework, which is delivered for the most part by our wonderful teaching assistants, under my supervision. The rest of the children in my class receive their curriculum entitlement on a two-year programme, which means adapting it to their current abilities and needs, depending on where they are in the cycle.

As part of the federation, the teaching staff each have an area of the curriculum that they are responsible for – initially this included creating a long-term plan for the subject and a carefully thought-out core knowledge document (which meant thinking deeply about what we wanted our children to know and be able to do by the end of each half term). Sharing out subject leadership across the four schools, though, has had a massive, positive impact on teacher workload, as so many teachers in similar settings can lead three or four subjects. This is complicated by most of our schools having only two classes with up to four year groups in one classroom! Having a Year 3 child in the same room as a Year 6 in some subjects can be particularly perplexing, especially in subjects like PSHE where the maturity and experience of each child is so wide.

Do you organise different subjects in different ways? How do you use other adults to support learning?

Yes, different subjects lend themselves more easily to teaching subjects as a whole class with appropriate adaptations, such as Music, Art and PE. I tend to teach everything else separately in varying ways! As I've already mentioned, Reception has their own curriculum and KS1 are taught together in the foundation subjects.

English is split between Reception and KS1, where the objectives are slightly different depending on which year group the child is in: for example, if I were teaching punctuation, the Year 1 focus could be writing simple sentences and full stops, while in Year 2 it could be more complex sentences, full stops and exclamation marks. Depending on where we are in the year, the Reception objective could be entirely different again! Until the end of this year in maths, each year group has been taught separately. While the Reception children accessed the continuous provision, the teaching assistant would teach the input for either Year 1 or Year 2 and I would teach the other one, then support the whole key stage during their independent work. This can feel like a juggling act at times, and I don't think I've managed to find the perfect solution yet! Next year, I want to trial teaching Year 1 and Year 2 maths together with year-specific objectives, while the Reception group will continue to get taught on their own... we'll see! Teaching phonics comes with its own set of challenges again: the teaching assistant teaches the Reception group, while I teach the other group. In the past, I have tried having three phonics groups with me teaching two of the groups, but this isn't always possible with other curriculum demands. A flexible or adaptable approach is often needed here to meet the children's needs.

Early reading is a key element of infant teaching. How do you manage this with children at different ages and stages?

Teaching children to read fluently is essential to any infant classroom, but particularly when it's mixed age. There are times, for example, when you may need a group to work on a task independently – this is so much easier if the children can read. Providing the children with the skills and knowledge to do this from when they start in Reception is vital if they are to become successful readers. What this looks like in practice is that I split my class into two groups; the teaching assistant teaches the Reception group while I teach KS1. Although I am obviously responsible for the progress of all the children in my class, it helps enormously that everyone who delivers the phonics programme is trained in it so that they understand the concepts behind what they are teaching, and the theory behind how the children learn. Good communication between me and the teaching assistant allows me to be able to assess how the children are progressing and put in extra support as needed. Teaching my group is a bit more challenging as I need to ensure that the Year 1 children joining me at the beginning of the year are taught the next steps they need, while ensuring that the Year 2 children are challenged appropriately, although for some it can be very useful consolidation as well. Regular formative assessment, as well as assessment for learning during the lesson, enables me to adapt my teaching to what the children need and prevent any potential gaps from widening.

Of course, reading is so much more than decoding, so ensuring that the children have access to the strands from the other half of the Scarborough Reading Rope (2001), is crucial.[3] Providing children with a text-rich environment is important too, as many of the children may not have this at home. I read to my class as much as I can, exposing them to a variety of texts and vocabulary. As they become more fluent decoders, they gradually build up their reading stamina and fluency. As soon as they start in Reception, I promote a love of reading and enjoy finding books that I know they will find interesting, everything from tractors to Pokémon.

Support from parents as their children learn to read is invaluable. I hold phonics workshops at the beginning of each academic year, so the parents know how to support their children. I talk about how the brain works in terms of working and long-term memory, as well as practical things like the importance of using pure sounds when decoding and what the phonics books actually look like. My aim is to empower the parents to realise the huge impact they can have on their children's learning, simply by listening to their children read for short periods every night.

What do you consider to be the benefits of mixed-age classes for the children in them?

I think the children gain a lot from being in a mixed-age class! The reception children quickly settle into school life as they are able to see what is expected of them from Year 1 and Year 2 children (who enjoy being positive role models), and the older children tend to take on nurturing roles by looking after the younger ones. The children make friends across year groups, which

---

[3] In Hollis Scarborough's 'Connecting early language and literacy to later reading (dis)abilities: evidence, theory, and practice'. In S. Neuman and D. Dickinson (eds.), *Handbook for Research in Early Literacy* (2001).

involves understanding on both sides – there is a lot of problem solving and negotiation that goes on in a mixed-age class! In terms of learning, the Year 1 children are exposed to whatever the Year 2 children are learning, which keeps expectations high. Also, being in a mixed-age class allows for a certain amount of flexibility as the children can be taught from whatever starting points they have. For example, a child in Year 2 who is working towards a certain objective can easily move within the class structure to make the progress they need to or consolidate some previous learning.

Do you think there are any benefits or drawbacks to teaching in a very mixed age class from the start of your career?

There are definitely more benefits than drawbacks to having taught in mixed-age classes from nearly the start of my career. When I first started at FitzHerbert, however, it felt a little bit like being thrown in at the deep end! Planning for three- or four-year groups at once was quite daunting, as my NQT year had been as a Year 5 teacher in a three-form entry junior school. I learnt a lot from colleagues about how best to approach it and was able to observe examples of great teaching in similar settings to mine. As a mixed-age teacher, I have become quite an expert in adapting teaching and providing necessary scaffolding to ensure all pupils make good progress. It also means that I know the EYFS Framework and the national curriculum of the whole of KS1. This allows me to see where each child needs to be by the time they leave Year 2, which is also immensely rewarding to see the progress they have made when they get there.

Teaching in a small school can be difficult when seeking out CPD opportunities as it can be hard to find cover within budget restraints. Although some professional training is provided by the federation, I have also sought out CPD in my own time, such as attending ResearchEDs and The Festival of Education, as well as completing some online courses. This has enabled me to keep up to date with evidence-informed practice, which I can then apply in my own setting to the benefit of the children.

What advice would you give to colleagues teaching in a mixed infant class for the first time?

Make reading a priority as it will make your life easier in the long run, as well as being hugely beneficial to the children's lifelong learning. My favourite thing about teaching this age group is seeing children become readers, especially when they have found it difficult to start with. It is a bit of a cliché, but it really does unlock the rest of their learning! Collaborate as much as you can with colleagues in similar settings as it can be quite lonely to start with. Shared planning is an absolute winner. Take advantage of the flexibility that teaching in a mixed-age class can offer. Think carefully about what will have the most impact on the children's learning and do that – this will have a positive impact on your workload. Get to know your children and their families as you will be working with them for at least three years.

Most importantly, enjoy it and embrace all the magic that an infant class brings!

LEARNING ACROSS AGES: MAXIMISING OPPORTUNITIES IN MIXED-AGE CLASSROOMS

A conversation with Jennie Gill

> Jennie is the senior teacher at South Darley CE Primary school. She has responsibility for the Early Years and Key Stage 1 class but teaches across the school each week. She loves living and working in such a beautiful rural area and embracing the challenges of small schools.

Please could you tell us about your role and the setting you work in?

I'm the infant teacher in a very small rural primary school in Derbyshire where I've worked for almost 20 years. That seems a ridiculously long time to have stayed in a single job, but when I look back on it I see that, while I may have remained in the same school, the job I do has changed immeasurably.

Being part of such a tight knit community is a privilege and an absolute joy and the continuity that it brings would be the first thing on my list of reasons that small schools are brilliant. And they really are brilliant! We know our families and our church community well (we're a Church of England school, controlled by the local authority) and there is a level of trust there that takes time and care to build but which allows us to work together and support each other. Often our school has educated the parents and sometimes grandparents of our current students and the families have deep roots here.

I have known three of my predecessors in my classroom and between us we span most of the past 60 years. They have passed on to me a legacy of respect and goodwill for the role that they worked hard to achieve. This level of 'knowing' and 'being known' in a community brings both great privilege and great responsibility. It wouldn't suit everyone, I don't think. You have to give the people in your professional life quite a lot of your personal self and allow them to know you well, too – it has to work both ways. It also means that you are working in something of a goldfish bowl, where any small issue is magnified and can be seen by everyone, so maintaining harmony and goodwill, even over the smallest things, is essential.

For the children it means that they have a smaller pool of children to play with and they have to learn to negotiate and get along as a group. They learn a huge amount about inclusion, working very much as a team to take responsibility for the younger children and those with additional needs. I love that our Reception children happily chat about their play at school and include the names of Year 6 pupils as their friends with absolute confidence. Our children know each other inside out, even down to identifying the smell of individual jumpers across the school! They also look after each other (in the words of our most recent Ofsted inspector, 'the children were adamant that bullying doesn't happen').

We have no room for passengers and everyone has to do their bit, otherwise we couldn't ever raise a sports team or put on a school show. The children also have to be accountable for their behaviour outside school because they are rarely out of sight of someone who knows who they are! They chat readily in the supermarket with ladies from church who come into school to hear them read and they know that all the adults around them value them, like them and want the best for them. As school culture goes, that's pretty powerful stuff, and culture is much more effective than any behaviour policy or strategy you could ever write.

How are your classes structured, and what do you find are the main challenges of your role?

Our class structure is variable. My infant (EYFS/ KS1) class has remained stable (so far!) and the juniors sometimes have two classes (Y3/4 and Y5/6) if numbers allow, and sometimes are one class with all four Year groups together. I teach full time and our headteacher job shares the Y5/6 class. When we have a third class, we are able to employ another teacher on a contract for a year or two. Often the third teacher is recently qualified and we like to think that we are able to impart some wisdom and experience while they certainly keep us on our toes with new ideas and innovations. We are all wearers of many hats as we share the areas of responsibility that would be the same in a school with a much bigger staff. I'm the senior teacher with a partial TLR and I am the named SENCO and the DSL. In practice, the headteacher and I fulfil both of those roles together the majority of the time. While I take on the bulk of the paperwork, with both of us having a big teaching commitment, it's good to be able to share the phone calls and meetings, depending on what else may be happening in school, as well as to have two of us doing the thinking in a tricky situation. I am also the collective worship co-ordinator and staff governor and I teach the RE throughout the school. This coming year, due to some unusually tricky timetabling, I'm going to teach Y3/4 science too, so there really is never a dull moment. None of the packed programme of work I do would be possible without the support of a talented and experienced HLTA who takes on lots of the day-to-day planning and resourcing of play activities, works with our EYFS children, runs interventions and will jump in to cover me at any point if something needs urgent attention outside the classroom. Our school is very reliant on our TAs, who are capable and adaptable and work well beyond whatever their job description might suggest that they actually do.

Teaching EYFS alongside Years 1 and 2 is complex, how do you manage this?

For the children to be in a class with children from Reception to Year 2 is, I think, a definite advantage, as long as you are willing to be (and encouraged by the headteacher to be) flexible enough to make it work. Sometimes we all work together as a class, especially in foundation subjects, with just a few tweaks for individual children's needs.

In literacy work, the Reception children tend to need their own adult-led time but the KS1 children can all work together quite successfully. In their writing in KS1, it's a similar range of skills that they are practising in each literary context but the older children will naturally extend themselves in the work they produce. In maths and phonics, I find it easier for my HLTA and myself to teach each of the Year groups individually for short sessions. While they may not have spent as long doing whole-class maths lessons by the end of the year as they might have in a single Year-group class, they will have spent all their maths time in a small group where they get lots of teacher attention and I can be sure they have all made progress in every lesson. While some of the Year groups are with an adult, the others can have access to the continuous provision which, for the older Year groups, might not be available in a single Year-group class. I absolutely believe that Year 2 children should have access to play provision in every class in an ideal world, but in our class it would be really cruel to have all those activities available but only for the EYFS children! This small group teaching model means that I can timetable everyone to have some free time to play every day, and listening in to conversations as they do so tells me that even the oldest children are using this time to explore what they have been taught as they role play and create craft projects. It means that Reception children with a good level of knowledge can easily have a go at a task I had in mind for KS1 and that older children with additional needs can access play resources or have a learning break without it being at all a big deal.

The small size of the school also means that the infant children see the juniors up close and have definite ideas about who their personal role model is. This year, for instance, they saw some stellar junior performances in the whole school Spelling Bee, and suddenly my Year 2 children had taken it upon themselves to make sure that they could spell like those juniors when they're older. The Spelling Bee was in October, and by Christmas they had almost nailed their Year 2 common exception words which really took the pressure off for the rest of the year!

How do you ensure that all of the children get what they need, both to meet the requirements of the national curriculum but also in terms of their next stage in education? Are there any benefits to this kind of class in terms of the curriculum?

We work together as a teaching staff to take responsibility for leading all the subjects. We have a file of evidence of the work we are doing to develop each subject and someone takes the lead on looking after it, doing work to include the voices of the children or adding helpful resources, but we focus on a subject each half term and all observe each other's lessons, develop curriculum and analyse assessment and progress together. It makes it a very supportive, collaborative process and means that all of us have a good understanding of everything that is happening. It also meant that when we came to re-write our curriculum a few years ago, in response to the new 2019 inspection framework, we were confident about what was needed. It did mean that we needed to beware of 'group think' and not get totally caught up in our own little bubble. We made sure that we had read research reviews for different subjects and looked at some models that other schools were using. What I'm about to describe is still a work in progress and curriculum is never really 'finished', is it? It's always evolving and hopefully improving. We had an Ofsted inspection last month and were pleased with how carefully the inspectors listened as we explained how our curriculum worked. They were happy with the breadth and depth of it and what it provided for our children. We make sure that our governors hold us accountable, too. They are an experienced bunch, several with an education background. They regularly come into school for learning walks and their quality feedback at the follow up meeting is always challenging but supportive.

For all subjects apart from literacy and maths, our KS2 children have always worked on a four-year topic cycle that all of KS2 work on at the same time. That's because four is the maximum number of Year groups that will ever be in the same class and means that, even when we have to change KS2 from one class to two, or vice versa, there isn't an issue with children having missed or repeated topics. In KS2, their literacy texts were and still are often related to their topic, but in the infants, although there is sometimes an obvious text to use, I find that it can look contrived if I try to link them all. The first big change we made was to put the infant class onto a four-year cycle, too. Although they will only be in the class for any three years of that cycle, it meant that we could match topics across the whole school and they would coincide every time we reach them. There were lots of advantages to doing this. We wanted to be clear about the intentions of our curriculum and this made it easier to plan a learning journey for the children through school that makes sense and tells a story. I picture it a bit like one of those brilliant open-top city bus tours you might go on when you're a tourist somewhere unfamiliar – people get on and off in different places and hear the information in a different order, but by the time you've done a whole circuit you all know the same facts and it has gradually come together to give you all a similar impression of the character of the city. It can also spark your interest in particular places that you want to take yourself back to later.

On a practical level, it means that we could share relevant resources and book whole school visits (sometimes we need to take everyone to make the cost of hiring the bus manageable). It makes it easier to remind junior children of what they know from a matching topic they studied in the infants because the next class of infants are currently working on it. And although we hadn't planned it specifically, the infant children have loved seeing that they do actually have a bit of knowledge about things they see the juniors doing. For instance, one of the infants stood up in our celebration assembly for doing a fabulous timeline of the life of Queen Victoria. 'Ooh, that's great,' said our Y5/6 teacher. 'We've been thinking about her too. Do you see that blob of blue tack on the door? That's how tall Queen Victoria was – wasn't she tiny!' The infant child beamed at being linked to work the juniors were doing and having a conversation point with the junior teacher. In that instance the infants' topic had been 'Kings and Queens', contrasting the lives of Queen Victoria and Queen Elizabeth II and looking at the monarchs in between, while the juniors were building on that previous experience to extend their knowledge of Victorian life and study the industrial revolution.

Additionally, in the RE curriculum, I taught the modern slavery units during that term, because you can't really teach children about the industrial revolution in Britain without mentioning that the whole thing was dependent on the cotton trade... and we don't grow cotton in this country. I often find that there is an RE unit that matches well with broader topics. The whole school learns about Jewish people and what they believe during the point in the topic cycle when the infants are learning about Remembrance and the juniors about the World Wars. In the juniors we spent several weeks enjoying learning about Jewish stories and celebrations and cooking some Jewish food in our RE lessons. Then there came a day when the children fell into the classroom, desperate to tell me that 'we know what happened to the Jews in World War 2!' Their history lessons had given them a much deeper understanding, and we then went on to look at the work of Rabbi Hugo Gryn, inspired by his father's stories of internment at the Lieberose concentration camp, and at how modern day Strasbourg, which changed from French to German hands several times in the twentieth century, acknowledges what happened to its Jewish population in very sensitive ways. The whole school visited the synagogue in Sheffield and were able to contribute to discussions with the Rabbi, who showed them scrolls and told them stories which they loved and still talk about across the year groups.

Other links between topics include the infant 'Nurturing Nurses' topic (Florence Nightingale, Mary Seacole, healthy eating, and talking to parents who work as nurses) while the juniors are working on the topic of 'Survivor' (Ernest Shackleton, building resilience, looking after mental health and getting ready for residential trips). There is usually a subject that naturally leads each topic and we have tried to vary these. We are also conscious that we want the children to understand the subjects as discrete disciplines, and so we have child-friendly definitions of each subject displayed in each classroom and draw their attention to which subjects they are studying in any given lesson.

Through the Diocese of Derby, we have been partnered with a slum school in Kolkata which several of us have visited over the past ten years. We definitely wanted to build that into our curriculum, and it appears for the infants as 'Beautiful India?' The question mark in the title was suggested by Debra Kidd in her book *A Curriculum of Hope*. It's a fantastic read and, in this instance, that question mark enabled us to celebrate all that we learned and loved about Indian culture and the children in our partner school while acknowledging the unfairness of the difficult lives those children lead. It was also after reading Debra Kidd's book that I started to include a moral dilemma to explore with the children towards the end of the topic. 'Beautiful India?' is one and it went well when I tried it. Later in the year we studied the Great Fire of London and used another of her dilemmas, reflecting on whether, if you found yourself in Pudding Lane on the night of the fire and found the first spark, you would choose to put it out. This proved very controversial and made the children draw on their knowledge of the impact of the fire and how the rebuilding had changed the city. As I write, we are about to start a topic 'Incredible Me!' and I am looking forward to a philosophical debate at the end about whether *everyone* **is** incredible. It's this kind of summative thinking that turns a list of teaching objectives into a meaningful curriculum. We have also tried to build into our topic work an increase in the outward-looking nature of the attitudes the children will need in order to engage with them. In the infants, we are focusing more (although not entirely) on ourselves and our place within our families and local community. The junior topics tend to reach further and encourage the children to be active in the wider world.

To be clear, not all of our topics line up across the school. We didn't want it to look contrived and there are places where the infants and juniors are working totally separately and we're very happy with that. Where they are working together, some of the links we make are deliberate and explicit, drawing on work from the previous term, or from the previous cycle. Others are incidental and made by the children. When we were doing some virtual tours of Hindu *mandirs* (temples) around the world, we came across a particularly beautiful one with mosaicked walls. As the camera rounded a corner, we were confronted with an archway covered in tiny swastikas and there was a collective gasp and look of horror from the children because they had previous knowledge of this symbol from their World War work the year before. I was taken by surprise also, but explained that the Sanskrit word 'swastika' means 'well-being' and the symbol had been used peacefully for thousands of years by Hindus, Buddhists and Jains before the Nazis misappropriated it. However carefully we might plan a curriculum, it's never going to find all the links because fundamentally it's life that overlaps in countless different places and in different ways for different people.

So far, creating our topic cycle seemed a big job but one which we were excited about. It was knowledge-rich and broad in its reach. But planning the skills development was a whole other thing. Some subjects specify skills for each Year group, others only for a key stage. Either way, we needed to be able to demonstrate a skills progression, even if the class had four Year groups working on the same lesson together. Our 'topics' are the contexts within which the children learn the skills and, while the topic cycle needed to last four years to prevent repetition, the skills cycle needed to be shorter in order to ensure that skills would be revisited and built upon. So, within the four-year topic cycle we built two shorter skills cycles. The skills that are taught in the first year of the topic cycle will also be taught in the third, and those taught in the second year will also be taught in the fourth. For instance, in the infants we develop our skills in sculpture when we design and make poppies as part of our remembrance topic and also, two years later, when we model shoes for Cinderella in our fairytales topic. Often skills are revisited more often but they feature at least every two years so that, wherever a child steps onto our open-top bus tour, they will meet and develop those skills in either Year 1 or 2, again in Year 3 or 4 and again in Year 5 or 6.

Are there any areas that you are still developing in your curriculum?

There are two areas where we are still a work in progress. One of these is the EYFS. Having reached a point where we are happy that we have a curriculum that fulfils the national curriculum requirements and the needs of our school, we are now in the process of creating a plan for each year for our Reception children. This is, of necessity, much more fluid and leaves more room for responding to children's needs and interests. But we are planning opportunities for play that complement the class topic and thinking about adult-led sessions where the Reception children will be able to join in with a whole class activity with just a few adaptations and others where they may need something different from older members of the group. And we need to make sure that the Reception curriculum visits each area of the EYFS framework each year so that the children are able to reach the Early Learning Goals. The other development area is assessment and how to evaluate the impact of our curriculum on the children's development. They are increasingly making links for themselves from things they have learned previously and they have the skills and the interests needed for their next topic; that much we can feel happening in the classrooms. We were also very pleased that our parent body told our inspectors last month that they felt that their older children who are now at secondary school had been well prepared. Each topic that we work on now has a vocabulary list that the children look through at the beginning of the topic and identify any word they already know. The definitions are displayed in the classroom and referred to as we encounter the words during our lessons. At the end of the topic, the children revisit their original list and try to add definitions themselves. They then complete a quiz at the end of a topic so that we can assess the knowledge they have gained. We also separately teacher-assess the skills they have developed in each subject. Keeping the two types of assessment apart makes it easier to demonstrate them and also to use them in the future. If I want to know how well a group of children achieved a particular geographical skill the last time they studied it, it won't matter about the learning context in which they learned it as the topic in which they are about to encounter again it might well be totally different.

One of the features of small school life is that you get to be involved in everything that's happening. Mostly that's a blessing but occasionally becomes a bit overwhelming. Developing this new curriculum has been a labour of love and we have sometimes wondered if it wouldn't be easier to buy in a scheme (which we have done for computing, although we match the units to our topic wherever there's an obvious link.) But someone else's schemes generally don't give us what we need, even where they have built in some mixed-age planning. What we have designed isn't finished and isn't perfect but it matches our school needs and context and enthuses the children and the staff. Developing it also means that the staff have hugely developed our own curriculum understanding and now feel ready for anything!

Are there any final insights you would like to share either for colleagues who are new to teaching multi-age classes or considering applying to work in a small school?

If I was going to give top tips for teaching in a school such as mine they would be:

- Be flexible. Within the curriculum and inspection requirements that apply, you need to be innovative to find ways to do what works and then be confident if other people point out that this might not be 'how things work in a bigger school'. It's true; it isn't. It's what you need to do for you and your children and that's fine. Be clear about why you're doing things and then stand your ground.

- Take the time to build actual relationships with all your stakeholders (children, parents, other staff, governors, church, neighbours, whoever else is part of your community). When you're going through a difficult time or you have a slightly 'off piste' idea that you want to try, things are so much easier if those people know and trust you. There's no shortcut to this; you have to put in the hours in the local community over a period of time, but when it works it's joyous, professionally and personally.

- Outside of school, keep your own interests and experiences as broad as possible. In a small school, where you have to be a jack of all trades, it helps to have a broad(ish!) interest in the world. One way to do this is to read, read, read. For a start, it's a good model for the children. Mine know that I like reading and that I've usually got my current book in my bag and they frequently ask what it is. It blows their minds that it's often something that our headteacher has lent me and we can then segue into a conversation about books the children have read and would recommend. (In that lesson where we were taken aback by the swastikas, I was able to react fairly smoothly only because I'd happened to read Sally Vickers' *The Librarian* in which elderly ladies sew the symbol into church kneelers, reclaiming it from the Nazis as an act of post-war defiance!) Not only that, but having outside interests is great for your mental health and helps you to keep a sense of proportion in the face of the very intense job you do. The children you teach have lives outside of school and you should, too.

There are certainly challenges and sometimes some creative thinking is needed but, in my experience, without hesitation, I would shout loud and proud that for children and for staff – small schools are BRILLIANT!

ADVOCATING FOR SMALL SCHOOLS: THE ROLE AND IMPACT OF THE NATIONAL ASSOCIATION OF SMALL SCHOOLS

A conversation with Neil Short

Neil began his teaching career in 1968 and worked in several schools across the North/Midlands eventually achieving three headships. From 2000 to the present day, he has worked in/visited more than 1000 schools across the country on a wide range of activities. He is presently working with colleagues from various organisations on ways to meet the challenges facing education at the present time.

Please can you tell us about your current role and your experience working with small schools?

My first headship was in a small school in the 1980s and I was able to visit similar settings in my two subsequent school leader roles. In 2000, I established my own company undertaking a wide range of activities, which led to an increasing involvement with small schools.

In 2002, I worked with colleagues from the National College for School Leadership (NCSL) on their two-year 'Leading Small Primary Schools' project. This in turn brought about a greater focus on this sector and I was able to use my increasing involvement to write a series of articles covering all aspects of school life from a small-school perspective.

This culminated in the awarding of a Churchill Fellowship in 2008, when I visited New Zealand to investigate the specific training there both before and immediately after appointment as a small-school head. Having worked on the

NPQH programme, I was concerned that there was no specific guidance for colleagues prior to appointment as the head of a small school.

I have visited many small schools across the country both prior to and following my appointment as Chair of the National Association of Small Schools (NASS) in 2014.

Can you tell us more about the work of the National Association of Small Schools?

NASS was established in 1978 and was originally called the National Association for Saving Small Schools (NASSS). This came at a time when many small schools were under threat of closure due to falling numbers. As this challenge faded, the association was able to change its name, omitting 'saving' and changing 'for' to 'of' to denote a sense of partnership (prior to achieving charitable status in 2016). Whilst still concerned to ensure that schools under threat of closure are fully supported, NASS has developed a wider role across the world of education: links and partnerships are now in place with a wide range of organisations, universities, and local authorities. The Association works alongside Ofsted and the DfE and is often consulted by the local and national media.

These links proved of great value when the *Small Schools Manifesto* was produced in 2022, which provides the future platform for enhancing the place of the small school in an ever-changing education world.

So as to gauge opinion, a selection of headteacher colleagues from across all regions of England were asked to respond to the questions below. Due to a short time scale, 10 heads answered and their responses form the basis for the conclusions drawn. In all instances, it is important to remember that the individual context of a school may go against the norm but these are the main areas of agreement.

What are the main challenges currently facing your members?

From the responses received, the number one challenge facing small schools at the moment is financial. Comments centred around having to do more with less, with schools struggling to manage rising costs with no rise in funding. These issues have a huge impact on all aspects of school life. The impact on staffing both in recruitment and retention was keenly felt. One colleague spoke of the problem of competing with supermarkets, as they were able to offer a higher salary with greater flexibility of working hours. Rising costs of energy and, for those who supply meals to other schools, the increasing costs of food, also impact upon the overall budget. One head reported that, 'Insufficient funding has become much more of a problem and we are facing a structural deficit now due to inadequate funding – the formula for funding does not support very small schools and the minimum funding guarantee is too low'. Some heads were compelled to provide financial support to their school through other means, with one head reporting that they became 'an official for a union to get facilities money to support the school as well as lecturing at a local university'.

Allied to this was the issue of SEND which was mentioned by at least half of the contributors. The notion of inclusion means that pupils who had previously been in specialist settings are now in mainstream school. This at a time when many parents actively choose the small school for pupils with additional needs as they perceive this would be the best place for them. Delays in receiving funding from the Local Authority and the reduction in the levels of support available all contribute toward additional pressure being placed on schools, with one head reporting that, 'SEND funding is a scandal (and as an inclusive school us paying the first £6k of each EHCP means we are penalised for being inclusive)'.

Curriculum and Ofsted were other areas of concern. The curriculum was seen as 'not fit for purpose' and 'in dire need of an overhaul'. The difficulty of having to cover a curriculum within a 2-, 3-, or 4-year age group was highlighted and the accountability of the same via the current inspection framework was also commented upon.

Perhaps the best response to highlight the issues of funding and accountability is the following: 'We are expecting a deficit budget for the first time next year, despite cutting staff and maintaining pupil numbers, having a good with outstanding Ofsted report and a glowing SIAMS inspection report.'

A testament to the resilience of the small school.

Have the challenges small schools experience changed over time?

Perhaps the key event over the past five years has been the Covid-19 pandemic. NASS utilised members to provide a commentary of how their schools and communities had been affected. The responses from colleagues mirrored these reports, with the following comment being an accurate summation of many contributions: 'The lack of respect from parents since Covid-19 [has risen as well as] families struggling with their mental health in the midst of the cost of living crisis. Small schools are a microcosm of what is going on in the UK'. Other colleagues reported that 'parental expectation has risen', while also citing that 'parental mental health has become an issue' and that 'increasingly we are called upon to support with health issues, parenting issues, parental conflict, marriage guidance, etc.', at a time when there were 'no support networks available'. This meant that schools have had to 'develop skills within [their] own staff team, and identify external providers to replace the support that was previously offered within social care'.

At the same time, the schools were still subject to levels of accountability via Ofsted, SIAMs and SATs. The changed Ofsted framework from 2019 brought about many problems both for small schools and for inspection teams to fully understand and come to terms with the specific school context. A working party, established in 2022 to iron out these problems, has gone some way towards resolving and easing these issues. Other schools developed ways to solve specific problems. One school faced with a falling roll situation opened a nursery, boosting the school population. At the same time, a bespoke curriculum was developed which attracted 'a lot of parents as they like our hands on creative approach to learning'.

A similar yet far wider ranging development took place in another school: 'We've adapted our curriculum to place a greater emphasis on outdoor learning, farm to fork, swimming, bikeability, road safety, dental care – we were noticing an increasing number of children entering school with a limited awareness of where our food comes from, how to keep teeth clean, safety on the roads and huge increases in children who are non-swimmers (could be linked to closures of pools during Covid).'

The role of the headteacher has also changed over the recent past and has had to adapt to the external pressures, with some heads reporting that they are 'teaching more', as well as 'leading residentials, trips, sports and driving the minibus'. Of course, all of these activities have meant an increased workload for the headteacher: 'Staffing has been tricky, this has meant I have needed to teach more. Although I love being in the classroom, it does mean that other things can't be done in the day and this then means longer working hours.' In turn, this raises questions about their own mental health.

The last word on the challenges of the recent past must be the following: 'Everything has got worse – there is little to no support networks available to schools as all public services have been decimated to the point of being almost non-existent. This means more and more pressure on schools – often feels like the last line of defence...'.

What impact has the expansion of multi-academy trusts had on small schools?

A Times Education Supplement (TES) article on 12 July 2024,[4] urged the government not to 'leave orphan schools to languish' and sought to gain support for small schools at risk of closure. This warning came from academy trust leaders who insisted the government look both at the funding structures for smaller primary schools and also at the financial support for trusts wanting to take them on.

This was highlighted when one of the respondents offered the following: 'The issue is very pertinent for me as one of my schools had a double RI ('requires improvement') and so an academy order. This has been a very worrying time all round. We thought we had found a home but have recently been told that the academy no longer wish to take us on.'

Of the other responses, only one school was at present in a MAT and found the arrangement of value for her federated schools, both financially and in her own role.

Three colleagues found that there was little appetite or pressure for their school to join a MAT. Another had been part of a collaboration of five schools until four of them joined MATs. Despite extensive research they have been unable to find a MAT that will meet their needs.

There has been discussion amongst colleagues at NASS Zoom meetings about the possibility of forming MATs which are comprised wholly of small schools. Barriers to this included the number of pupils required to become a MAT and the costs involved.

One school provided a detailed description of the process and concluded that 'MATs for small schools do not add up'. In contrast, a small-school cluster decided to take the first step along the MAT route and the process is expected to begin in autumn 2024. This was due to the lack of support from the local authority, the best option in terms of sustainability, and also being a means of maintaining autonomy.

All in all, a mixed picture.

The TES article gave evidence from trust leaders about the viability of small schools and few solutions. The notion of small-school hubs as mentioned within the article bears some consideration and is working effectively in some

---

4   www.tes.com/magazine/news/primary/small-primary-schools-need-urgent-support-labour-government-mat-leaders

trusts. It may be the way forward. What must be understood and digested is that small schools offer ways of working which are effective and successful. The skills and qualities required of teachers working in mixed-age class (at minimum two years and often more) are often not fully understood and may be dismissed. And yet they are vital in ensuring the small school remains a viable and effective educational resource for their community. This article also mentioned some research which indicated that 'at the current rate of academisation, all schools will not be part of a multi-academy trust until 2041'. A response from one colleague in the survey highlighted the difficulties facing the small school: 'It has led to less support from the LA and confusion about the direction we should be heading in. There is no spare time to research the various options or lack of options we have as a very small school'.

In a time of falling birth rates, do you have any advice for small schools who are facing declining pupil numbers and the possible threat of closure?

The TES article mentioned previously spoke of 'falling pupil rolls' and whilst this may have been an issue nationwide it was not a major concern for those who responded to the survey. Of the 10 responses, four announced that they were oversubscribed. Reasons for this varied but included: that the school provided an alternative offering for those children whose parents were concerned about their ability to cope in a larger environment; another that about being heavily subscribed and having to turn away 20% of parents who wished to join the school (which is often overturned on appeal); while parents from another school spoke positively about the experience, attracting others to wish to join.

All respondents found that it necessary to ensure the school was making efforts to attract new children, which included ensuring that there were 'constant publicity opportunities'. One school opened a Nursery to build numbers and took the NOR (number on roll) from 41 to 63. As seen previously, one changed the curriculum to one which features outdoor learning, inquiry-based learning and pupil's voice heavily in order to attract parents. A federation of schools made more creative use of staff to became more innovative in subject leadership.

As noted in the introduction, NASS is still concerned to prevent closures of small schools, and will support all schools when this is threatened. Our major role in this process is to ensure that the correct procedures have been carried out throughout the whole process. At the same time, there is a recognition that closure may be inevitable. The pandemic highlighted for NASS the value of the small school within its community and the innovative ways that schools have developed to guarantee their future intakes needs to be commended.

Finally, were there any other concerns raised by the respondents that you found noteworthy?

Some of the broader issues included: getting new pupils to school in an area which is sparsely populated and requires a car to make the journey; how the variation in numbers are regarded to make a school viable within local authorities; the increasing numbers of high-needs children, the funding required to support their needs, and the risk of deficit budgets; one school spoke of being rejected by an academy trust due to future pupil numbers; and one head spoke of intending to retire in two years, but worried that it would not be possible to replace her, leaving her three schools vulnerable to closure.

In conclusion, the *Small Schools Manifesto* indicated that they were 'assets, centres of innovation in education and communities and treasuries for their localities', which are qualities that this small-scale research has highlighted. However, being head of a small school is a demanding role, where 'the headteacher doubles up as SENCO, DSL, LAC Designated teacher, Pupil Premium Coordinator, Assessment leader and subject leader for several subjects which is on top of a 0.45 teaching commitment – leading to a feeling of needing to be in several places at one time. It is a demanding job without the time and money to take a breath. It is also quite unhealthy because of the time spent tied to a computer. Family time and time to pursue interests outside of school is a problem, given the workload'. NASS will continue to support schools and individuals wherever and whenever required.

STEPPING INTO LEADERSHIP: EXPERIENCES AND INSIGHTS FROM A NEW LEADER IN A SMALL SCHOOL

A conversation with Michael Allen

Michael Allen is the senior lead teacher at Middleton Community Primary School, a small school in Derbyshire. He currently teaches a mixed-age Year 5 and 6 class. In addition to being the designated safeguarding lead, Michael also leads Maths, Physical Education, and Computing. This is his second teaching post, having previously taught in another rural primary school within mixed-age classes. Michael has completed his NPQSL and is currently undertaking his NPQH.

Please can you tell us about your current role, your school, and the class that you teach?

I am the senior lead teacher at a rural school in Derbyshire, which currently has 95 pupils on roll and encompasses a range of responsibilities across the school. My role includes being the DSL and curriculum lead for Maths, PE, and Computing. The school has 29% of children on the SEND register and is slightly below average for Pupil Premium. The school is organised into four classes: Reception/Year 1, Year 2, Year 3/4, and Year 5/6. Teaching in the Year 5/6 class gives me a unique oversight of the progression throughout the school, which is invaluable when discussing future curriculum development.

My current class has 33 children with a wide range of needs. I regularly lead the school and thoroughly enjoy my role.

Why did you choose to begin your career teaching in small schools, and did your teacher training prepare you for this?

Having attended a small school myself as a child, I was fascinated by the sense of community and the ethos of such schools. One of my earliest school memories is of my headteacher sitting on a dunking stool at the school summer fête, with children eagerly queuing to throw wet sponges at him. That image stuck with me– it reflected the values, attitudes, and selflessness of the staff who participated in the wider school community.

From the moment I decided to teach, I knew small schools were where I wanted to be. There's something special about the commitment, collaboration, and unity of a small school. Staff and pupils work as a team, tirelessly ensuring the school thrives. Each small school is unique, with its strengths and areas for development. From my experiences in five small schools, I've found passionate staff committed to broadening children's experiences and delivering a well-rounded education both inside and outside the classroom.

Unfortunately, initial teacher training didn't adequately prepare me for the realities of working in small schools. While training can only offer an overview, it fell short in equipping me with practical skills. Training modules often clung to outdated methods – like differentiated outcomes or lollypop sticks for questioning – rather than empowering teachers to adapt and be flexible in their practice. Many relevant topics, such as working collaboratively with parents or addressing the impact of the online world on children's resilience, were underexplored.

I completed my teacher training via the Schools Direct route, which allowed me to spend 37 weeks in the classroom. Unlike the PGCE route, this was invaluable, as it let me experience the importance of building strong relationships from the start of the academic year and adopting a collaborative approach. My training in small schools offered a clear view of the demands placed on staff. I was fortunate to have exceptional mentors who guided me through the rewards and challenges of small schools, giving me opportunities to lead whole-school events.

What particular experience does working in a small school give colleagues who want to progress to leadership quickly?

Working in a small school means you take on responsibility from day one. In my first teaching role, I was responsible for computing, online safety, and later, online learning during the Covid pandemic. These experiences allowed me to hone my leadership skills, including supporting staff across the federation and local schools. It gave me a clearer vision of my career aspirations.

In small schools, fewer staff often means more responsibilities for each teacher. This provides invaluable experience in leading, coordinating, monitoring, and reviewing on a whole-school level – opportunities that may come much later in larger schools. After only three years of teaching, I became a senior leader, overseeing curriculum areas and serving as the designated safeguarding lead. With a supportive headteacher and highly skilled colleagues, we've been innovative in creating inclusive practices and developing a curriculum that enables children to thrive.

How do you balance the responsibilities of being both a classroom teacher and a school leader?

Every day is different, and balancing these responsibilities can be far from straightforward. On average, I lead the school one day a week, but this fluctuates depending on my headteacher's commitments and safeguarding needs. Despite the challenges, the rewards of working with the right team make it worthwhile. I am fortunate to have a dedicated team supporting me in leading and improving the school.

While leadership responsibilities can mean time away from teaching, I've worked hard to establish routines that ensure continuity for children across Key Stage 2.

Are there particular challenges to managing both teaching and leadership in a small school? If so, how do you overcome them?

The biggest challenge is time – time to teach, plan, prepare, lead, and focus on school improvement. By establishing consistent routines that help children feel secure and adapting the curriculum to make it engaging and manageable for staff, we've been able to lead proactively.

Another challenge is the capacity to complete tasks with integrity, as teaching staff often have increased responsibilities. In small schools, teachers are rarely *just* teachers, which requires balancing multiple demands while working on school improvements collaboratively. Space constraints can also limit provision. The SEND crisis and increased behavioral needs have further stretched our resources, making it difficult to provide sufficient space for dysregulated children.

Additionally, parental accessibility has become more challenging in recent years. With the rise of technology and online gaming, the demands of supporting parents have grown significantly.

Sometimes there's a perception that leading in small schools is just a stepping stone, leading to frequent leadership changes. Do you agree, and how can stability be achieved?

Schools need stability, and unfortunately, not all small schools have this. I know of schools where 'SuperHeads' have come in without understanding the community or context, stayed for two years, and left the school in a worse state. On the other hand, some schools have had long-standing headteachers who, despite past successes, have struggled in recent years.

Small schools offer an incredible opportunity for teachers and leaders to make a lasting difference. In the age of multi-academy trusts, small schools need consistency and support to thrive. Staff should be given the flexibility to adapt the curriculum, collaborate effectively, and dedicate time to development. Improved collaboration and shared resources between schools could also foster stability.

What advice would you give to teachers in small schools considering leadership positions while continuing to teach?

Pay attention to the small details, remain adaptable, and embrace every opportunity you're given – you'll have plenty!

GLOSSARY OF ACRONYMS AND ABBREVIATIONS

CIAS Communications, Interaction and Autism Service
CPD continuing professional development
DBE Diocesan Boards of Education
EHCP educational health and care plan
EEF Education Endowment Foundation
EHE elective home education
EHT Executive Head Teacher
EYFS early years foundation school
ITT initial teacher training
LA local authority
LAC looked after child
MASH multi-agency safeguarding hub
MAT multi-academy trust
NASS National Association of Small Schools
NLE National Leader in Education
NPQEL National Professional Qualification for Executive Leadership
NPQH National Professional Qualification for Headship
NPQSL National Professional Qualification for Senior Leadership
OECD Organisation for Economic Co-operation and Development
PISA Programme for International Student Assessment
PKC Primary Knowledge Curriculum
SBM School Business Manager
SEND special educational needs and disabilities
SENCO Special Educational Needs Co-ordinator
SIAMS Statutory Inspection of Anglican and Methodist Schools
TLR teaching and learning responsibility